WANT TO
PUBLISH A BOOK
LIKE THIS?

BMD PUBLISHING HAS PUBLISHED DOZENS OF BOOKS LIKE THIS IN NUMEROUS BUSINESS SECTORS.

OUR PROCESS IS EFFICIENT AND EFFECTIVE.

IF YOU'VE ALWAYS WANTED TO DO A BOOK BUT DIDN'T KNOW WHERE TO BEGIN, GO TO *WWW.MARKETDOMINATIONLLC.COM/BMDPUBLISHING* TO SET UP A FREE *TURN THE PAGE* CONSULTATION.

BEGIN AN EXCITING NEW CHAPTER IN YOUR LIFE!

IT'S YOUR TIME TO BECOME
AN AUTHOR

Whinypaluza

Inspiring Adventures in Parenting

Rebecca Greene
LCSW-R

ACKNOWLEDGMENTS

I dedicate this book to my husband Seth and our three children; Max, Ella and Lillie. You inspire me every day! You are all my dreams come true! If the four of you enjoy this book, then it was all worth it. There wouldn't be a book without Seth encouraging me to publish this. I also must thank my parents. They were my real teachers who taught me how to parent! They also support me every step of the way. I would also like to thank Market Domination and BMD Publishing. My book wouldn't exist without your amazing expertise! Just like it takes a village to parent, it takes a village to get a book made. I am a blessed mama!

INTRODUCTION

I started writing my *Whinypaluza* blog because I wanted to document my life for my children. I hoped my children would enjoy reading about their childhood. It was all going by so quickly and I wanted to write it down to look back on. Parenthood goes by in such a blur.

Somehow, I now I have a 12-year-old, 10-year-old and six-year-old. I feel like it was just yesterday they were babies. My purpose for writing shifted from writing for documentation and memories to becoming my greatest coping strategy for parenthood. I find when I get all my feelings out onto paper it makes me feel so much better. Go try it! I get lost in my writing and feel my stress melt away. Sometimes I read my blogs over and over again as a way of getting over a situation. I also get requests now from my children on what they would like me to write about. That feels awesome when they ask me to write about their birthday or something else that's meaningful to them. "Are you going to write a blog post about our trip?" Ella asked me. She also asked if she could write a post herself. Both my mom and mother-in-law have made requests for me to write about a certain topic. My friends have also started making great suggestions. I love topic requests!

When my husband told me he wanted me to make my blog into a book I was hesitant at first. I feel as though I am baring my soul to all of you. However, I quickly changed my tune and agreed to the book, because I felt it could help people. I hope to relate to you and show all of you that we are all in this crazy world of parenting together. I always describe parenting as the most magical and most exhausting adventure. Thankfully I have an awesome husband to do this with me. I couldn't do this without our fabulous village of our parents and our friends helping us along the way. I feel very blessed that we live near all our parents and that we have such a great community of friends.

As a student I studied parenting, social work, sociology and psychology. Those subjects were all calling to me. It doesn't matter how much you study something, and it doesn't matter how many families I counseled, because there is always room to learn more and to grow more. My kids teach me this lesson every day. Just when you think you have figured your child out they decide they need something different from you.

You are going to hear a lot about my husband and my children. My husband keeps busy running two businesses. Market Domination is his marketing business and Silver Spoon is his financial planning business. When I gave birth to my son Max, we made the decision that I would stay home with our children. Max is a sixth grader who is very bright and gets awesome grades. He is also on a travel soccer team and is a fabulous goalie. Ella is in fourth grade and is such a diligent hard-working student. She also takes acting, singing and dancing classes and dreams of being on Broadway. Lillie is in first grade and is having such a great school year. She just keeps climbing reading levels and wants to read everything she sees. Lillie also does gymnastics and dance classes. The girls both do Girl Scouts and all three kids go to Hebrew School. I keep busy as one of the Presidents of the PTA where my girls attend school and as a troop leader for both Girl Scout troops. I also have three fur babies that keep me busy. Our black and white kittens are Faith and Joy and our golden retriever puppy is Tanner. You will hear about them too.

I am hoping you will laugh with me, cry with me, and let out some of your stress as you read through this book. I know parenting can feel like a roller coaster sometimes. Buckle up and get ready for the Greene family. If I don't cover a topic that you are feeling you need help with, you can always contact me to write about it or for a personal session with me.

Enjoy!

Laughing, Loving, Learning,
Rebecca Greene, LCSW-R

TABLE OF CONTENTS

SLEEPING BABY

Trying to put Lillie down for a nap is so hard! I have a small ranch and loud children. I had tripped and broke my monitor, so I leave the door open so I can hear when Lillie is up. Where is that new piece for my monitor? It better come today!

I am trying to rock my very tired baby. First Ella comes up to me screaming to get a hair off her tongue. Then Max starts screaming from the bathroom to come wipe him (Max you are six, wipe yourself). I put Lillie in her crib and wipe Max. I come back to Lillie wide awake. I tell her it's nap time and walk away. Now she's crying, and if you know me, you know I won't let her cry. It's back to the drawing board. Now I have a tired cranky baby and the four and six-year-old are as far away from me as they can be, giggling very loudly. I settle Lillie down, get her sleepy again, rock her, and put her back in her crib.

Now one of our three cats is scratching at the bedroom door. Seriously, Lillie gets no peace and quiet. I grab the cat and throw him in the living room and then run to the front door because Max's friend is now banging on the door. I guess the sign I put up that Lillie is asleep means that it is okay to bang hard on the door and wake her up. I tell Max's friend he will be out to play in a few minutes and then run into the kitchen because Max is opening and slamming the fridge looking for more food. How many times can Max eat? Now there is chicken all over my floor. Seriously Max, you can't wait five seconds for me to get you a piece of chicken! I calmly clean up the chicken (I will admit that I swore quietly a few times) and then give Max some chicken (not the chicken from the floor but trust me he wouldn't care). It has now been 45 minutes of Lillie sleeping and I am completely exhausted from trying to keep my house chaos to a minimum. Oh no, here comes Max's friend again! I need to get him outside. In summary – I need a bigger house and I need my wonderful kids to go back to school. I just love nap time!

KIDS AND THEIR STUFF
BY SETH GREENE

So, my wife got mad the other day.

I was trying to help, as usual, and somehow managed to screw it up....again.

The tornadoes named Max and Ella had gone through our playroom and dumped toys all over the floor. I was enabling them by cleaning up after them.

Then it got worse. I found out I wasn't following my wife's organizational system for the playroom.

It went sort of like this:
Me: What is your organizational system?
My Wife: I have one.
Me: What is supposed to go in the middle drawer of the second plastic cabinet to the right of the dresser?
Wife: Max's stuff.
Me: Does Max know about this? Here's how that conversation might go, honey. "Hey Max, where does your stuff go? Oh Daddy, Mommy says my stuff goes in the second drawer. Do you put your stuff anyplace else? Nope Daddy, only in that drawer."

Conversation stops because my wife just peed her pants – so we wait while she changes her underwear.

Wife: That was not funny.

Me: Another pair of underwear says it was. And you don't have a system.

Wife: Yes, I Do. Max has a crate for his stuff, Ella has a crate for hers, and Lillie has one.

Me: So, you've educated our 10-month-old daughter about where her stuff goes?

Wife: Okay, fine! You're not here every day. You don't understand what I have to deal with. I've got stuff everywhere! I am trying to maintain some semblance of order here, and survive my days, and then you come home and mess with my mojo!

Me: Your system.

Wife: Yes.

Me: For dealing with all the stuff you have to deal with.

Wife: Yes. Now do you understand?

Me: Uh...put stuff where it goes?

Wife: Yes, is that so hard?

Me: Not if Monica from Friends came by and labeled everything.

Wife: I could do that!

Me: The thought of you with a label maker scares me.

Wife: Just put the stuff where the stuff goes!

SNEAKER HELL

For some odd reason I decide to venture out with all three of my kids to buy them sneakers. I had heard from a couple of friends to head to a particular store so off we went. First, I couldn't find it, so I drove in circles for a while among crazy back-to-school shopping traffic. We get into the store and Ella finds Barbie sneakers that she loves. Of course they are too small and they don't have her size. She doesn't want any other sneakers, until she finds Smurfette ones and only has eyes for them. They are not at all what I would pick for her and I am not sure they fit, but whatever.

We go down Max's sneaker aisle and he takes down every pair of Skechers to try on. After trying on four pairs, he figures out that only one pair has an off-on switch and that is the only one he wants. Please oh please for the love of G-d have his size! I flag down a woman who makes Max try on the 13.5, 1, and 1.5, and finally she decides that the 2 fits him. Max has now tried on about eight pairs of Skechers, Ella has tried on five pairs of sneakers, and Lillie is now in her stroller screaming. I grab my children and run to the checkout – get me out of sneaker hell!

It won't be easy to leave because the line is out the door and there is only one cashier. I'm waiting in this very long line, Max and Ella are dancing around bumping into people, and Lillie is still screaming in her stroller. I pick up Lillie and send Max and Ella over to the front window to sit down and wait for me. They are now crawling in circles aggravating each other. Ella is obsessed with Max's new sneakers and keeps turning them on and off. Max is screaming and Ella is laughing while annoying her brother. 10 people later, Lillie is falling asleep on me, and it is finally my turn in line. The woman won't check me out without seeing Max's sneakers. Are you kidding me? "Max come here please. Max come here! Max get over here, take off your sneakers and please show the lady so we can leave!" She asks me if I would like to buy socks too as they are buy one get one. Oh yes, can I please get out of this long line and go look at your socks? No way, lady. Check me out so I can leave! I finally leave sneaker hell with one pair that I know fit my son and one pair I bought to shut my daughter up so I could get out of there. That is almost two hours of my life I will never get back!

WALMART

Why Walmart?

I decide to run out alone with Ella to a couple stores. This will be easy, right? Wrong! I run into Walmart, which I think will only take me a few minutes. Oh, how I crack myself up! We start by grabbing some chips and baby food. We then go look to see if they have *Teen Beach Movie,* which my kids are begging me for. No luck but Ella is screaming that I buy her *Fairytopia*, the Barbie movie. "No way Ella be quiet, sit down, let's move it!" We bump into a friend that I haven't seen in years and proceed to catch up. Every two seconds Ella is asking if she can talk. "I went to see Smurfs 2. It is a great movie. Have you seen it? You should take your son. How old is he? Vexy is my favorite Smurf." My sweet friend is humoring Ella and all I want to say is "Stop talking about the Smurfs and let me get two words in!"

Ella starts complaining that I promised her we would look at Barbies, so off we go. "Now Ella, you are picking a Barbie for your friend's birthday, not for you." This should be fun! I escape the Barbie aisle with the present I need (okay, and a $3 littlest pet shop for Ella. Just call me sucker mom). I then remember I forgot to get baby gifts and a folding table. "Can we leave yet? Can we leave yet? I want to go home!" Ella is starting to whine and get loud! I grab baby gifts, a card, and a folding table and book to the checkout while Ella continues to whine. Oh Walmart, you have the slowest and longest lines with the slowest cashiers! (This was before self checkout). Remind me why we came here? Ella opens her littlest pet shop and plays with her new toy.

I look down at my phone. Oh no, we have to get to Ella's school picnic! "It's okay to be late, it's okay to be late," I continue to tell myself. Oh no, the head of Hebrew school is texting me. I text her back letting her know I will get the (late) forms done. I missed a few more texts. I can't always respond right away to people and that's okay! I can't keep up, and yes I am still in line. I finally get to the car and unload my shopping cart. Oh no, I never checked for Barbie sneakers for Ella! That is why I brought her. That was my main reason for running out to stores with Ella. I told Seth it would take five minutes. Oops! $100 later I head home. Cursing Walmart, I say I will never shop there... till the next time. Now I need to go order *Teen Beach Movie* and Barbie sneakers online and I need to go fill out the Hebrew school forms. Check, check, and yes, we made it to Ella's school picnic! A mom's life isn't easy!

NURSING

The love of Breastfeeding:

If I hear one more person tell me not to breastfeed, I think I might explode. I can't quite understand why people think they can interfere with intimate details of your life like breastfeeding.

I understand they are looking out for me or judging me or whatever. Let's talk about breastfeeding. My son was born, and I was determined to breastfeed him after all the research I read about how good it is for your baby.

I was a first-time mom who had no clue what I was in for. Sleepless nights breastfeeding a starving little boy every two hours became my life. He was and still is a vulture. I was an exhausted mess and my little angel of a son kept making me bleed!

The lactation consultants tried hard to help me in person and on the phone while I cried. I got to the point of, "Don't let this vampire near me!"

When you are crying and bleeding you know it is time to throw in the bloody towel (at least for me). I turned to pumping, and then felt like a cow for the next nine months.

Thankfully my daughter Ella nursed easily. When she latched on and it didn't hurt, I couldn't even believe it! Years later I found out from my sister in law who is a chiropractor that Max needed his tongue clipped. This wasn't a big thing back then. If he had his tongue fixed, I bet breastfeeding him would have been a lot easier.

I was so happy and now could see how moms could deal with breastfeeding their babies. This is how it should be. This is okay. I can do this!

I got so excited that I forgot to introduce a bottle and found myself stuck with a baby who won't drink out of any nipple I buy. Trust me, I tried every single nipple out there!

My reality became that I had windows of opportunity to leave, but then would get phone calls that Ella was screaming and crying, and I would rush home. "This is okay, I can do this," I would tell myself, and then wonder, "Why won't this baby let me have a life?"

Nursing your baby through a cold is not fun at all. I kept suctioning her nose trying to help her breathe so she could nurse. For the love of G-d Ella, take a bottle! Ella was now 17, months old and on her third cold!

I looked in her big beautiful blue eyes and said, "I am so sorry honey, Mommy can't do this anymore." That was the end of breastfeeding Ella! Call me a good mommy for doing 17 months, call me a bad mommy for cutting her off, but I knew at that moment that I was done. The funny thing is, Ella knew too, and she seemed to understand... or so I hope!

Now my daughter Lillie is nursing. Okay, I learned. I started pumping and nursing and giving her bottles and nursing. I made her flexible. I learned from my mistakes.

Every month I give myself a pat on the back. I am feeling so done!

My baby is almost eleven months old. We will see how this goes. Weaning sucks! Literally.

I want to drink a glass of wine without feeling guilty. I want to drink a huge cup of coffee. I want to go out at bedtime and have Seth or my mom be able to put Lillie to bed.

I want my boobs back! I want my body back!

There are women who whip out their boob in public and nurse with no problem. Kudos to them. I am too shy for that. You have women like me who hide while nursing, and there are women who don't want to nurse or can't do it. Bottle feed, breastfeed, cow feed, goat feed, whatever you want, just let people do what they want with their own baby!

Be flexible, be accepting, be less judgmental, and help your fellow women get through this joy of motherhood!

Now go feed your baby. I am going to go nurse my baby and figure out this whole weaning thing again!

LEAVING THE HOUSE

My goal for the day was to grocery shop, and be home and unpacked by 4:30, when I needed to take Max for a haircut. Doesn't that seem reasonable to you? Just wait! This was before Instacart days. Where was Instacart when I had babies?

My cleaning lady is on her way over so guess what I start doing? Yes...cleaning! I do the dishes, I clean up all the toys, and then I begin feeding and getting the kids all dressed. The cleaning lady shows up and then Lillie decides it's time to go to sleep. Now she can't vacuum, and I can't leave the house!

Lillie decides to take a very long nap. Now Ella and Lillie are hungry for lunch and I can't find my son. He was just in the front yard. Oh Maxwell, you are supposed to ask before you go in someone's house!

I feed the girls and am now stressing about what time it is. I find Max next door and ask my neighbor to send him home. Ella is telling me she wants to go swimming with Grammy (my mom) and Max is screaming that I always take him away from his friends. I get suckered into leaving Max with my neighbor and I rush to drop Ella off to go swimming and run to Wegmans. Why do I think I need to please my children?

I zip through Wegmans as quickly as I can. My cart is so heavy (we were out of everything), and Lillie appears to be falling asleep again. The girl takes forever to load my cart (they are usually fast, she must be new), and I decide to do drive-up to make my life easier.

I book to my car, book to the line to get my groceries and watch the man slowly unload all my groceries into my trunk. I rush home and unload my groceries as quickly as I possibly can, grab my son from the neighbor's house, then drive all the way down Transit to get Max's haircut at Capello's by my best friend Liz. How I made it on time is beyond me, but I did it!

I am getting text messages from my husband, my mom and my realtor, Lillie is crying, and I am trying to have a conversation with Liz. This is just so much fun! Max's hair looks awesome by the way.

I run home and feed the kids and myself dinner. Thank you, Mom for sending food home with Seth and Ella (Oh yeah, Seth picked up Ella) and run out the door to Ella's school meeting. I sit through the meeting and then I am off running again.

I pull up and Lillie is crying in a stroller outside with my neighbor, Ella runs into the house, and I see Max hysterically crying inside. Seriously people, I was only gone for an hour.

I calm down Lillie and then go inside to see what is wrong with Max. What a day. All I wanted to do was leave the house!

MAX'S FOOT INJURY
BY SETH GREENE

My wife had to go to a Universal Pre-K meeting at my daughter's nursery school.

She left me with all three kids.

Two of my neighbors show up and ask if they can take Lillie for a walk around the block in her stroller. I say yes, one down.

Then they offer to take all the neighborhood girls in the driveway with her, and Ella agrees to go. Two down.

They are going to leave me with all the boys (five total). The boys ask if they can do timed (stopwatch app on iPhone) relay races on the lawn.

I say sure as this will keep them busy (and not fighting with each other), and me seated for a while.

Max takes his Crocs off. Says they slow him down. I tell him to put socks and sneakers on if he wants to race. He refuses. One of the neighbors tells Max to put shoes on. He refuses.

Mistake #1.

The neighbors and all the girls leave.

On his third barefoot race, Max runs over the jagged edge of a neighbor's drain in their lawn and starts screaming.

As Max hurts himself all the time, I don't race over to him, I walk over. I figure he will cry for five minutes and be fine.

Mistake #2.

I pick his foot up and it has blood dripping down it. Not one drip at a time, but it's running down his leg and my arm.

I pick him up and carry him into the house, into the bathroom. I'm not thinking clearly, so instead of going into the kitchen and grabbing paper towels, I grab one of my wife's favorite pink towels with Ella's name on it and press that on his foot.

Mistake #3.

Max is screaming bloody murder. He sucks when there's blood involved. It totally freaks him out.

I pull the towel away to look at the cut and clean it. Max sees the blood all over his leg, my arm, and the towel and the floor and starts screaming louder. "Daddy take me to pediatric urgent care! I don't want to die!"

Did I mention that Max can be a little bit dramatic?

After about two minutes the blood stops. I cover it in Neosporin and bandage him up, carry him to the living room, and put him in the chair with an icepack.

His friend's pound on the window at least three times to see what's going on as they saw him get hurt and can hear him screaming.

I yell at them not to pound on the window that my wife broke doing the same thing a few weeks ago. I think I might have scared them off.

The chair isn't working for Max's foot, so he moves to the living room floor. I would ask him to try not to bleed on the carpet, but I don't think he can handle much right now.

I give Max a TV show, a drink and a Pop-Tart to help calm him down, so I can clean up the mess.

I clean the kitchen floor that our cleaning lady just washed, I clean the bathroom floor, the sink, and change his shorts.

He is still crying, in between the juice and the Pop-Tart. I cuddle him on the floor. He asks me if I ever had a cut so bad, and how I survived. "How long did it take before it stopped hurting?"

After about 45 minutes, I remember that the neighbors still have both my daughters. I should probably get them back before my wife shows up and wonders what happened.

I text them and they say they still have my daughters and will bring them right back.

At that moment Lillie decides to start crying in the stroller, and my wife pulls up.

She comes home to a crying hungry baby, a still crying injured son, and a stressed-out husband.

Luckily, Ella was fine. She just wants to know why Max got a Pop-Tart when he didn't eat all his dinner. I give Ella a Pop-Tart to shut her up.

Of course, now my wife wants to know what happened, so Max has to relive the whole thing and start crying harder all over again now that Mommy is home.

Is it bedtime yet? Is there a sippy cup filled with vodka in the fridge?

Thank G-d my mother-in-law bought me both Jack Daniel's and Absolute Vodka gift sets for Father's Day.

MAX'S BIRTHDAY PARTYPALOOZA

My son is turning six. Time to plan the dreaded birthday party!

Max currently has a million friends and wants to invite every single friend and have a huge fun party, which his father's wallet doesn't enjoy.

Seth hears us making the birthday list. He comes over and says to us, "You only get 20 slots!" 20 people? Is Seth crazy? I was at 35 trying to get it down to 30. This should be fun!

Seth then lectures Max and I that instead of crossing people off he should have found out how many slots there were first and then only let Max pick 20 friends.

Man do I hate when my husband is right!

Well, there are 20 kids in Max's class so we can't invite the whole class. We have neighbors, we have good friends, and we have class friends. Wait till he starts to get Hebrew school friends and sports friends. The list is always so fun!

Somehow Max and I get the list to a little above 20 and Seth okays it. We now start fighting about where to have it. Seth and Max both vote for the Buffalo Museum of Science, so I am outvoted. Fine, the Science Museum it is.

Now on to setting a date with the Science Museum. Check! Picking a room at the Science Museum. Check!

Ordering a cake. Check! Ordering the food. Check! Buying favors. Check! Decorations for the room. Check! Is my list complete?

We text the cake lady a picture of the Angry Birds cake that Max wants. She shows up at our house with the cake and she is not happy about what she charged us, for how hard this cake was. Seriously lady, you could have called us and said you needed to charge us more. You could have called us and said the cake was too hard and we needed to pick something else. People are funny! This was before the fabulous friend we use now to make our special cakes.

We load the kids, the cake, the favors, the diaper bag etc. and off we go to try to be early for Max's birthday party. Max is off-the-wall excited, and Ella is complaining about wanting to plan her birthday party.

Seth and my dad wheel the cake up to the third floor. Why did I pick the third floor? I didn't need the nice brand new room on the third floor. Mistake #1!

I enter the room and there are decorations up. They told me there wouldn't be. I didn't need to buy decorations. Mistake #2!

The kids start to mill in one after another, filling up the room. Why did I invite so many kids? Mistake #3!

Let's get started Science Museum and keep these kids busy!

The Science Museum did an amazing job keeping the kids entertained. The problem was, once the woman was done with her experiments, the kids were bored. "Where is the food? Let's go!"

The food shows up, and the brilliant mom I am, I let my son order chicken fingers and chicken wings. Everyone is looking for the pizza. Uh oh, mistake #4!

It gets worse. The plain chicken fingers we ordered seem to have a mild sauce on them and kids are complaining. I am now at mistake #5!

Is the party over yet? Let's get the cake done and get everyone out of here.

I am overstimulated and overheated, and my husband is staring at me like I am crazy. "Leave me alone Seth!" I mean, "I love you honey!"

Now my boobs are throbbing, and my mom is in the corner giving Lillie a bottle. After attempting to pump in the party room (silly of me), I run downstairs, find a private mom room, and finally get to pump and feel better. Huge kudos to the Buffalo Museum of Science for the private mom room and for the great birthday party. My family and I love the Science Museum.

This was a crazy day and it isn't over. Everything is loaded in a few cars and we are off to go home and let Max eat more cake and open a ton of presents. On the ride home, Ella is now beyond jealous and begging me to start planning her birthday party, and Max is already asking me where he should have his next birthday party. Partypalooza baby!

SCHOOL

I just finished writing a letter to Max's first grade teacher, which is inspiring me to write this. School with Max so far has been anything but easy.

I started putting Max into preschool at age three. My friends all told me he would love preschool at age two, but I know my son and I strongly disagreed, and chose to wait until he was three. I probably should have waited until he was four! Don't let people rush you!

I would take Max to school every Monday, Wednesday and Friday morning (for 2.5 hours of school) and Max would cry and cling to my leg. I would encourage him, keep a straight face and then book to the car crying. I never showed Max one tear, but boy did I cry that year! The teacher and my friends who volunteered in his classroom told me he was fine once I left and was just giving me a show. I wanted my son to love school so much that he would run away from me forgetting I was there.

The following year for UPK was no better. I was hopeful. Max is older and will have an easier time being way from me. Not so much luck. Max cried almost every day of UPK telling me he didn't want to go, and he wanted to stay with me. This is what I get for doing this to my own mom! I pawned off driving Max to school on Seth as my emotional state couldn't take it anymore. Yes people, I am the sensitive mom. I married my husband for a million reasons, he is absolutely perfect for me!

One of those reasons was because he had no problem taking Max to school and dropping him off. I don't know if Seth knows to this day the degree to which that helped my emotional state.

Somehow Max and I made it to Kindergarten. I begged the school for a sweet, nurturing teacher and explained that I didn't care about academics. I just want my son to learn to love school. I don't care about reading, math, sitting still, the rules, etc. I just want my son to love school! I know how smart Max is, I know he will be fine academically, let's get his emotional well-being doing better at school.

Max loved his Kindergarten teacher and I didn't have to fight with him every single day to go to school (only sometimes). I kissed the ground, I kissed Max's school, for the first time my son was not crying every single day about school. Part of this may be that Max is getting older and more mature and getting used to going to school every day. Whatever the reason, I don't care what it is, I am a happy mama!

Now summer is coming to a close and I am holding my breath about first grade. I asked again for a sweet and nurturing teacher and again said that I don't care as much about academics. Oh, how the teachers are going to love me! Max is reading above grade level – great! Max has made a lot of friends – great! Max is a joy to have in my class – great, great!

All I can say is does my son love school, and that is ALL I care about at age six. Wish me luck for a smooth ride through first grade with Max!

HOUSE HUNTING WITH CHILDREN

Seth and I have been house hunting on and off for about six months now. Seth is not so happy with me that I haven't picked a house yet.

However, in my defense, I have tried. My husband has also been all over the place with how much money he wants us to spend on our next house.

The first house I wanted had a bidding war and we couldn't afford to bid over some of the other bids.

The second house had someone who already put their bid in and really wanted it and I wasn't feeling it to compete over this house!

The third house had another big bidding war and the person who bought the house paid full cash. How am I supposed to compete with that?

The owners of the fourth house were crazy with what they were asking. We put a bid in for what we thought it was worth, and went back and forth, but the bottom line is, in our opinion it is not worth what they want for it.

There are plenty of houses that Seth liked and would live in. I am trying, I really am. I have also told myself I shouldn't have to try. When it is the right house I will know.

I am sorry Seth! Better to feel tortured now then for 40 years hearing about your wife not loving her house.

I can't even tell you how many houses we have seen. Our realtor has shown us houses and I try to go to open houses frequently on Sundays.

My parents and neighbors have been wonderful and very often we leave the kids with them while Seth and I run to a house.

I am also doing more and more by myself because Seth has had it and I don't blame him. Honestly, I have had it with myself.

My goal was to have moved before school started, and here we are at the end of August and I am still searching for the right house for my family.

In my opinion you need a patient realtor who will put up with you and your family! Thankfully my realtor puts up with us. Max and Ella run up to the door and scream and fight over who is going to help open the lock box. Max did the last house so this time it is Ella's turn. The next fight is over who is going to turn the key to open the door.

Seriously can we just go in and see the house?

When we get into the house, the next battle is which kid is going to go with which adult as I am not allowing my children to be free in someone's house. Who knows what damage they could do?

Max is already up the stairs. My kids love stairs because we live in a ranch, so it is a novelty to them.

"Max you need to come downstairs and start in the kitchen with me and you actually need to stay with me," I yell from downstairs. I try to control my rambunctious six-year-old and keep him from touching everything and running around enjoying the space in the homes we see.

I am lugging my eleven-month-old daughter around the house, up and down the stairs. Max is right behind me and Ella has clutched onto my realtor and won't let her go.

We head into the basement. This is Max's favorite part as he has to test the basement and tell me if there is enough room for him to run. I love when he says no to a house because the basement is too small. He cracks me up. My husband asks him if he is paying for it. "If you aren't paying for it you don't get a say!" I yell at Seth to be nice, but quite frankly he has seen so many houses, how can I ever give him a hard time?

By the way, Seth has flown through the house in his two-minute fashion and has already decided that I won't like it. He wants to leave and go to the next house. I know he is right but of course I want to look!

The upstairs is terrible, and the bathrooms are majorly outdated, the carpets all need to be pulled out and the master bathroom is a closet. Seth was right and I wasted more time.

I am ready to move to the next house and start booking down the stairs as I have seen enough. My kids are obsessed with finding the door in the floor (a story my mom made up and told them, so now they look in every room for this door), and Max and Ella are still going through the bedrooms. "Let's go kids!"

I continue to go down the stairs and now hear my realtor asking if what Max is doing is okay. He has now decided to walk down the stairs on his hands. "Max, how does that seem like a good idea?" I ask my silly six-year-old to please use his feet to walk down the stairs. The things we have to say as parents. Did you think you would ever have to tell someone to use their feet to walk downstairs?

He gets to the bottom and then decided to run back up so he can do it again, but I grab his shirt and pull him to me. "Max, it is time to leave and we don't play on stairs," I scold him as I wonder why on earth I brought him with me.

I turn around and Ella is now screaming about how high the stairs are. "I'm afraid of heights, this is too high, I'm not coming down!" I am very frustrated as I have two more houses to see, and this one is putting me over the edge.

"Ella, take the railing and slowly walk down the stairs. Let's go," I ask her as calmly as I can get myself to ask. My realtor comes up next to her, grabs her hand, and slowly walks her down the stairs.

I am now feeling sweat pour down my back, and I'm completely frustrated that the pictures online looked so nice. I look at Seth and apologize and tell him he doesn't have to come to the next round of houses.

On to the next house. Only two more for today!

At the next house it is now Max's turn to help with the lock box, Ella's turn to turn the key, and Seth's turn to lug Lillie up and down the stairs.

"Now kids, you stay with me in the next house, you walk slowly through the house, and you calmly go up and down the stairs," I lecture them. Seth makes up a good behavior contest to see who can behave the best in the next house.

"I will find a house. This will all be worth it. Everything is okay." I continue to give myself a pep talk. The joy of house hunting with kids. Remind me to leave them home next time! My advice is not to take your husband and children house hunting. Find a house and then bring them to check it out!

HOLIDAYS

Holidays are so fun!

The Jewish holidays are here. Rosh Hashanah is next week. The first week of school! Are you kidding me? Doesn't the Jewish calendar understand that the first week of school doesn't work for me!

Seth's parents are divorced which makes things even more fun than usual. After almost 30 years of marriage they decided to get divorced.

The phone calls and text messages begin about planning the holidays. I tend to do it at my house or my parents' house because both are "neutral" grounds.

The other issues are dietary. My parents eat extremely healthy and my dad is on a special diet. Seth has certain things he can't eat. Then there are my kids, who want basic foods with no sauce, gravy or spice to it.

Seth's mother asks me if my family wants to come to her house for Rosh Hashanah.

Thank you, thank you, I would love a break! Will my parents come and be able to eat, and will Seth's dad and his girlfriend come?

It is a Jewish miracle. My parents say they will go, and Seth's dad says he will go. Step one accomplished!

There are two dogs at Seth's mother's house. This should be fun with a little girl who screams (Ella is afraid of dogs) and a baby who crawls.

I explain some menu issues to Seth's mom and ask her to please let me know the menu when she plans it. I am that annoying parent, but I need to see if there is stuff for my family to eat, or I would be glad to bring stuff they will eat. No casseroles, no gravy, they won't eat any of that stuff!

We have a date. We have a place. Let's do this!

ELLA GOES TO THE EYE DOCTOR

I was four months late, but I finally made Ella an eye appointment before she goes back to school. I drag Ella to the car, while she is yelling that she wants Daddy to take her. (You and I both know that if Seth was taking her to the car, she would be screaming for Mommy to take her. Sometimes she just wants to be difficult.) "Just get in the car. We're late!"

We sing songs from *Pitch Perfect* the whole way to the eye doctor and then run through the door. I am late... but only a little!

I don't know why I rush to any doctor's appointment, because they are always at least a few minutes behind. I really need to learn to slow down.

Ella's eye doctor is awesome! She loves him, and he is so good at his job. Dr. Gordon brings us in and asks me right away if we have been doing the eye patch. That is Seth's job. He does it every day.

Uh oh, there is more. "What does Ella do with her eye patch on?" She colors, plays with Play-Doh, and plays with her Barbies. Uh oh, wrong answer! I later find out Ella needs to be outside with her eye patch, riding her bike, playing with balls, rocks, etc. (Mental note: better get on that!) Dr. Gordon gives Ella the homework assignment to get outside and show off that patch.

Ella is giggling away during the eye exam, and Dr. Gordon thinks she is a trip. She loves the chair going up and down, she loves the bright lights and she thinks the doctor is so funny.

I am laughing away because Ella keeps giggling. He asks what the picture is. Ella says, "A bee." He shows her again and Ella says, "It's a bee!" He shows her a third time and Ella rolls her eyes, looks at him like "Are you serious?" Ella answers again with "IT'S A BEE!"

I am now trying to stay on the chair and not pee my pants! "Is she always like this? Or do I bring this out of her?" I respond with "She is always like this, but you definitely bring it out." Ella is a goofball who is always happy and always giggling.

Other than laughing, I am holding my breath. I am nervous about the results of the eye exam and scolding myself for taking so long to come back. The results are in...Ella's eyes have significantly improved, and I am beyond thrilled and relieved!

We have come a long way from the pregnant mom who couldn't stop crying in his office because I found out Ella couldn't see well out of her right eye. We had taken Ella to another eye doctor before Dr. Gordon, who examined her and said she would grow out of her eye turning in, and that it was no big deal.

My advice to all you moms and dads:

1) ALWAYS follow your instincts. I knew in my gut that something was wrong.

2) Make sure you go to good doctors. Talk to people and get recommendations. A second opinion is always a great idea!

We don't need to come back for six months. Woohoo, great news!

Ella now remembers that I promised a Paula's donut afterwards, so off I go to attempt to find it (I always have trouble finding it). After about 15 minutes I give up and look it up online. My husband laughs at me and doesn't understand why I "try" to find places, when my phone will TELL me.

I find Paula's and it is closed, and they've relocated. Ella is now begging me to go find the new place. So, we find the new Paula's, and my happy girl gets her donut. That is, happy until she finds out it is time to leave and go race to go look at houses.

My baby can see well! I couldn't be happier! Her crying about not wanting to look at houses doesn't faze me as I know now that she is seeing the world around her.

PREGNANCY NUMBER ONE

My husband wanted to be married a few years before we got pregnant. Was he kidding me? I was about to turn 30 and I was having major baby fever. I lectured him about how old I was, and that we wanted a few kids, and I didn't want to be old when we had our third child. I explained that he didn't understand because men could have babies forever. Seth quickly learned he was fighting a losing battle!

After nine months of marriage I was pregnant. Seth was happy and totally freaked out too! He had no idea what a fabulous father he was about to become. He started telling me he was never changing a diaper. He said he had never held a baby. My thoughts in my head were "Whatever, Seth. Think what you want. Yes, you are changing diapers, just be quiet already." I was a good wife, and I just listened, and kept in my head the thoughts he is now going to see published!

While I was pregnant, I was supervising social workers doing family therapy for children with serious behavioral problems. I would drag myself to Lockport every day, park in the parking lot, and make the walk up to my office. I found myself feeling very cranky and I couldn't seem to get enough sleep. I was running to the bathroom a lot, and all the social workers were becoming suspicious of my moodiness. For several months, I would come home, make dinner, eat with my husband, and then say goodnight as I couldn't keep my eyes open. Note to self: you can only do that with your first baby everyone!

When I announced in a meeting that I was pregnant not one of them was surprised. They were all hoping there was a reason for their supervisor turning into "Cranky leave me alone" supervisor! I'd better shape up. I didn't want to be known that way. At least now they had a reason.

As my feet and ankles swelled up, I continued to drag myself from the parking lot to my office. I started to get major back pain every day, and work was becoming more and more difficult. My wonderful doctors kept asking me if they needed to sign me out of work, but I was determined to push through, which was a bad choice. I didn't want to sit home and be bored. Little did I know boredom was soon going to be a thing of the past and I should have been lying on my couch enjoying my last days of freedom!

I am now 38 weeks pregnant and at my doctor's appointment. I know a few of the doctors really well but today I was seeing one who didn't know me well. I explained my major back pain. I said I couldn't keep working and begged her for a medical excuse. She examined me and said there was absolutely no sign of the baby coming, and that I should probably go back to work. Noooooooo! I couldn't do even one more day. I begged and pleaded. Finally, she did sign me out. Then my friend from work called me a sissy! The pain was unbearable, and as it turned out, my back pain was labor!

That night the labor pains really began. Seth and I headed to the hospital and were ready to meet our baby girl. Oh yeah,

Seth talked me into being surprised (the one and only time). I had been having a ton of baby girl dreams and was ready to meet Hannah Rachel Greene. So, I thought!

24 hours later I was on my third hour of pushing. Excuse the graphic details, but Seth is running away because he is totally grossed out by all the blood coming out of me. I don't care, I say, "Get this baby out of me!!!" My wonderful doctor used the forceps, the vacuum and did everything she could possibly think of to try to get Max out. I was so frustrated because I could see his head. All of a sudden, I'm being wheeled to the operating room to have a C-section at hour 25, because my baby was in distress, (which they didn't tell me). I'm arguing, "I am not having a C-section, let me push, please let me keep pushing!" The next thing I know, they put me out, as they needed to get my baby out quickly! My poor husband was left in the dust wondering what was going on!

I wake up and my throat and belly are throbbing, and I'm wondering, "What did they do to me? Where am I?" I see my parents and Seth standing over me and I am totally disoriented and in tons of pain. "This completely sucks! This is nothing like I thought it would be! The miracle of pregnancy, the miracle of birth! This all sucked!" Now I've been cut open, which is exactly what I tried to avoid. I had a vision. My vision didn't happen.

My parents go home after seeing the baby and I and knowing that we're okay. Seth is telling me his parents left after meeting the baby, and the baby is okay (I guess they weren't worried about me). We had a boy. A boy! What was he talking about? All I could think was leave me alone. I was a complete mess from the whole ordeal, and I didn't care about anything!

I wake up at 4 a.m. in a complete panic! Where is my baby? It was at that moment I had the realization that my baby was no longer inside me and was off somewhere. I needed to see my baby that instant or I was going to lose it! They wheeled him in, and I grabbed him. My baby boy! Nine months of pregnancy, 25 hours of labor, and he looked exactly like his daddy! Too funny! I do all the work and he looks like Seth! I stared at my baby boy for hours and cuddled him. I never wanted to let him go. Okay, now I get it. I finally see the miracle, and at this moment I am completely content!

Maxwell Joseph Greene, it is a complete honor and joy to meet you, I am your mom!

P.S. I could barely move, and Seth changed all of Max's diapers the first week of his life!

MOMMY BRAIN
BY SETH GREENE

I would like to address the phenomenon I call Mommy Brain.

Here's how I imagine my wife's Mommy Brain works.

She goes in the kitchen to finally feed herself (after feeding three kids breakfast, it's almost time to think about lunch).

She notices that there are dishes in the sink and on the counter. She does the dishes. She finally gets to the bottom of the sink.

She thinks, "I've got a clean sink, I should bathe Lillie in it." She goes to the bathroom to get the bath supplies. She notices the laundry on the floor.

She moves the clean laundry from the dryer to the basket, the done laundry from the washer to the dryer, and starts a load of laundry in the washer.

She notices the basket of clean laundry that needs to be folded. She takes the basket of clean laundry into the bedroom to fold it. She folds the clean laundry. She puts the folded laundry away.

While putting Max's clean, folded clothes in his dresser, she notices there are some clothes in the drawers that don't fit him anymore. She starts organizing all of Max's clothes.

Lillie crawls into the bedroom and wants to nurse. She carries Lillie into the kitchen in one hand, while washing her nursing shield in the other.

She sees the clean sink and realizes that she never ate anything, or bathed Lillie. She yells at herself that she can't ever get anything done in this house.

We have come full circle, and that's Mommy Brain.

I HAVE AN ADDICTION

I need to confess something. I have an addiction. I have been keeping this inside for way too long.

Seth has been helping me cover this up. I need to get this off my chest. As a social worker I know the first step is to admit you have a problem.

Hi, my name is Rebecca, and I am a people pleaser!

I know there are a lot of you who are going to relate to this one. I want everyone in my life to be happy with me and with each other.

I was the peacemaker in high school who went on to be a social worker.

People ask me what I was like as a teenager or as a child. "Did you give your parents a hard time?" Ha! I laugh and think about how I always wanted my parents to be happy and proud of me!

I was focused on that. I wanted to make their life as easy as possible. G-d forbid I ruffled any feathers!

The people pleaser goes on to get married and have children and the addiction continues. I get lost in the whirlwind of my day and making my family happy.

I make sure my family is fed. "Didn't I just give them breakfast?" I make sure they are all happy. "You want a $75 new Wii game? Okay honey, I will talk to daddy."

I fix toys. "You broke this for the 50th time? Okay, I will glue it again and again." You lost your Barbie? "Don't worry I will look for it again, even though I tell you every day to keep her in the same spot."

Max wants to invite friends over. "You want 10 friends over and I just cleaned? Okay Max."

I try to do errands without my kids. "You want to go to two different places to avoid grocery shopping? Okay, kids. I don't mind running around!"

I turn off reality TV and check in with my husband. "I haven't had a moment to myself all day, but Seth what can I do for you now?"

I repair cuts, scrapes, bruises and kiss all their boo-boos. "You got hurt wrestling after I told you to stop? It's okay, come here honey."

Your glasses are dirty again? "Okay honey, let me clean them again."

You want to nurse again? "I haven't eaten or drank anything yet today but let me nurse you again."

I listen to all their problems and empathize, and problem solve. "You guys can't learn to be nice to each other? Okay, let me listen again to who did what and try to help."

Can't you work out your own stuff?

I help with homework. "How is this kindergarten homework that I don't understand?"

I cook meals. "Really didn't I just give you lunch?"

I do their laundry. "Stop wearing clothes!"

I run them to activities. "Who signed you up for all this stuff?"

I help my husband with work stuff. "Oh yes honey I have plenty of time to make work calls for you."

My friend needs to see me. "Sure of course, any time."

My friend wants me to join the school board. "Of course, I have so much extra time."

The list goes on and on....

I sit down for a few seconds here and there and think "uh oh, did I eat anything?" Oh yes, I ate Ella's leftover mac and cheese! That was when Seth called me from his lunch meeting eating salmon. How is that fair?

The days fly by like a whirlwind and I lose myself in the fabulous chaos. I thrive on chaos and taking care of my family.

However, I look down at my nail polish half off and remember the days my nails looked beautiful. I look in the mirror and see my roots growing in and wonder when the last time is I got my hair done. I look down at my thighs and scold myself as I need to take time to work out.

It is fabulous to take care of your family and friends but remember to schedule time for yourself! How are you supposed to be a good mom and wife if you have nothing left to give? Don't you deserve a manicure? Yes, in fact I do!

Guess what? Not everyone is going to like you and it is okay! Not everyone is going to be happy with you and it is okay!

There were a couple of friends that we had when Max was little that decided not to be friends with us for different reasons. My mother taught me as a child that jealousy tends to be at the root of these issues. I have also found that sometimes friends just grow apart or that I just don't get along with certain people. When my friends like someone that rubs me wrong, I used to ask myself what is wrong with me. Now I realize that I don't have to like everyone. I also realize that everyone doesn't have to like me. I need to focus on the people who love me for me and surround myself with people who make me happy.

The older I get the less I care what people think. By the time I am 40, maybe this addiction will be a thing of the past.

Today I am going to confess to the world and myself about my people pleasing addiction! Today I am going to do something for myself! I am going to sit here and do my nails and tomorrow I will make myself a hair appointment!

It's a step. I need to be a good example for my kids. I want them to take good care of themselves!

WHY IT TAKES THREE DAYS TO WATCH ONE TV SHOW

BY SETH GREENE

I write this after giving up and turning over the TV to my children in frustration.

My wife and I are stupidly trying to watch television while the kids are awake.

Having made this mistake in the past, I am prepared. I have asked the two older kids if they are hungry. They both said no. My wife is nursing on the couch, so she's got the baby covered.

The older two have toys to play with and appear to be happy. Silly me. We start the 30-minute show.

Then my son decides that he IS hungry and wants my leftover steak from last night.

I was going to finish it after the show, but whatever. The other day I was literally putting a fork IN MY MOUTH and he says, "Daddy, are you going to eat that?"

Yes! I am going to eat my own food that I PAID FOR! My wife is way too nice and makes me give him the food off my plate and I have to eat something else.

So, I went in the kitchen and cut up the steak. I microwaved it and served it and sat down to finish the TV show my wife and I had been trying to watch for the last few days.

As soon as I sat down, he asked for juice. I told him to wait for a commercial. After three minutes he went to the kitchen and helped himself to some juice. Thank G-d for small miracles.

Except G-d has a sense of humor, and my son manages to spill the apple juice he is pouring for himself all over the kitchen floor.

I pause the show again and go in the kitchen to clean up the mess.

Now that the floor is only a little bit sticky (I will finish it later), I give him a glass of juice (after he cries because I made him eat at the table vs. in the living room where he wants to eat), and try to go back to the show.

We got halfway to the next commercial break before he asked for more steak.

This is why it takes us three days and several hours to get through one show that's less than 25 minutes of actual TV time.

After he's fed again, we turn the show on again. Then my son crawls under a clear plastic crate we were using to pack up toys to put in our crawl space because we don't have a basement and our house is exploding. My four-year-old daughter holds the crate down and my son who could easily push his way out freaks out and starts crying.

So much for trying to watch TV.

If only we could ignore them!!

MAX'S FOOT INJURY PART II
BY SETH GREENE

So Max is having a fit because he wants to go to his friend's house, but he won't wear socks or shoes over his cut up foot. He says it's uncomfortable.

We're trying to protect his foot from dirt and infection.

He says, "You don't understand what it's like to have a cut like this," as he's throwing himself against the wall. "And I'm not going back to school in socks!"

My wife, who's a germophobe, says, "You think I'm going to let you walk around that filthy school barefoot?" She is so mad at him, but I keep telling her this is comedy gold.

She starts laughing. Then Ella says, "That's why it's called Whinypaluza!" My wife has to run to the bathroom before she pees her pants.

Max is throwing things and crying. Ella explodes, "Whinypaluza all over the place!"

"Are you going to stay in the house and cry all day?" I ask. "I'm not going to wear any socks ever again!" Max insists. He's on the ground crying, punching the floor and kicking.

It's going to be a great day. I can just tell.

DADDY'S HOME

Some days fly by and Seth shows up. Some days drag and I count the minutes for Seth to get home.

There are days I have had enough, and I just want to run away. Even to Target for an hour. Somewhere away.

It is 4:30 and I give myself a pep talk that Seth will be home in an hour. I can do it!

The minutes drag and I start to make dinner with Lillie hanging on my leg and Max whining because he is so tired. At least Ella is happily playing with Play-Doh.

I hear Seth's car door and jump for joy! He runs through the door all happy from a good day at work.

Max comes up to him and starts whining about his day and everything that has gone wrong.

I see my husband's smile change to annoyance in less than five minutes. Seriously, I have been here all day!

Why does Seth think he can act like this? He has been gone all day! Shouldn't he be patient, kind and loving? Well, Max continues to be upset, and Seth quickly puts him into time-out.

Max doesn't stop whining so Seth sends him into his room.

Max doesn't stop so Seth now tells him to go to sleep. Max now comes up to me hysterically crying about how mean Daddy is.

Oh yes, Daddy is home!

PREGNANCY NUMBER TWO

The first pregnancy I asked for. We had our son Max and I fell in love with my little boy.

Max was and is a mama's boy who wanted his mommy all the time.

Seth would joke with me that he wanted a daddy's girl and kept saying he was ready for number two. "Are you crazy?" I would say. "I am not ready! Give me a few more months and we will talk. I am the one who has to do all the work.

Oops! Guess what? Pregnancy number two!

I am so nauseous, and I throw up multiple times every day. I am a stay-at-home mom, so I am thankful I don't have to go to work and throw up there!

I am listening to my friends complain about their weight gain, and I find myself concerned that I can't eat, and I can't gain weight. Who thought I would ever be concerned with weight gain?

I plead to my doctor, "When will the nausea end? This better be a girl! If another boy is putting me through this, he is in serious trouble already!"

My doctor kept telling me the nausea would end soon, and

the doctors all predicted a girl because my pregnancies were so different.

After hating the surprise of my first birth, I tell Seth I am finding out what this baby is!

We head to the doctor to find out. In my mind I am seeing myself with all boys. Seth's dad had a brother, Seth has a brother, and Seth and his brother each have a son. "The Greene men make boys," I would tell myself.

They do a sonogram and tell me it is a girl, but I don't believe them. They look again and tell me it is a girl! I am not convinced but I am excited.

The nausea goes away and I go back to normal. I am chasing Max and trying to keep up with his energy all day.

We take him to Strong Museum, and I lug my big belly through the whole museum. I go grocery shopping and lug all my groceries home. I proceed as normal because I don't know any better!

Slow down pregnant mamas! Keep those babes cooking!

When you are pregnant you can't hold your bladder. You sneeze and you pee! You cough and you pee! You laugh and you pee. It sucks!

When I went to bed that night and woke up with fluid coming

out of me, I ran to the bathroom thinking the pee had a mind of its own. The pee won't stop! I'm so confused. It isn't pee!

I scream, "Seth! My water broke!" We run to my parents, drop off Max and run to the hospital. I am not ready for this!

We get to the hospital and the nurse wants to make sure my water broke. "What are you talking about? The water is still coming out and you have to do a test?" Sometimes medical people make no sense to me!

I tell her to do her test because she doesn't believe me, and she confirms, yes, my water broke. Thanks, Einstein!

Now they start planning for the delivery. "Delivery?" I scream, "Keep this baby in me!" When they told me I had to deliver my little girl I was beside myself. I was six weeks early and I wanted her to cook longer!

"Why did I go to the museum? Why did I grocery shop? Seth should have done the grocery shopping!" I am royally mad at myself.

Since then, I have heard I could have made them monitor me and keep Ella in longer. Who knows if that was the right option?

They start prepping me and ask me if I want to try a VBAC (vaginal birth after a C-section).

Seth is behind the nurse shaking his head no. Okay, I

understand it is his child and wife here, but seriously, he thinks he gets a vote?

I know in my heart that Seth is right (darn it), so I give them the go ahead for another C-section. I'm not happy at all to be cut open again for the second time.

However, I am beyond excited to be awake this time for my baby's birth! I have no idea what to expect, so I am a nervous wreck, but let's do this!

Note to all you mothers getting C-sections – tell them you are nauseous. Tell them you can't stop shaking. There are meds for that during your c-section.

After some serious nausea Ella is delivered! They show her to me and then explain she has to go right to the NICU to be checked out because she is so early.

Are you kidding me? First, they put me out after 25 hours of labor with Max and now they are taking Ella away from me! This totally and completely sucks!

Severe shakes are next for me, to add to all the fun. I stop shaking and get wheeled to my room.

They tell me I can't go see Ella. I demand a wheelchair and to be brought in to see my baby.

There are tubes all over Ella and they are giving her a feeding tube! Good Lord give me strength! I cry and cry, and the nurses look at me like I am crazy!

I leave and come back and cry and cry and the nurses look at me like I am crazy!

Ella is in the NICU for eight days and I cry, and cry and the nurses continue to think I am crazy! They had to teach her to eat. They had to get her sugar level and jaundice under control. It was a long 8 days.

Yes, I will admit that I am crazy. I want my baby!

I am supposed to be taking care of myself. I am supposed to be lying down. I am supposed to be pumping every three hours around the clock to give my baby breast milk.

I just want to be with my baby!

Somehow, I got myself through those eight days. My husband was my rock. My mom, who had Max all week, would call me on the phone at the hospital and tell me to enjoy the down time. My life was about to be crazy, and she wanted me to rest up. I just wanted both of my babies with me! In retrospect she was right, and I should have been relaxing. My life would soon be busier than I had ever known!

Leaving the hospital without my baby on day 7 was so extremely hard for me. They told me I couldn't stay any longer and that Ella wasn't quite ready to come home. I was told that I could call her at 6 am to check to see how she was doing the next day. I slept with Seth and Max all night and held Max and cried. I cried because I had missed Max so much. I cried because I was home without my baby. Life wasn't as it should be yet and I was a lump of sadness.

I woke up the next morning and called the hospital right away. They gave me the good news that Ella's numbers for her jaundice were good and that I could come pick her up. My sadness quickly turned around and I couldn't get to the hospital soon enough.

The morning I got to take Ella home I began to feel like a normal person again. "Ella Rae Greene, welcome home! We are through the moon excited that you are healthy, okay, and ready to be home." You gave your mom quite a scare Miss Ella!

Now when I ask my four-year-old why she came so early, she says routinely "Because I couldn't wait to see my family!"

I love that girl!

By the way, Seth got his wish and got his daddy's girl!

ELLA'S QUESTIONS
BY SETH GREENE

Why didn't we buy Aunt Carol's pink house?
She's not really your aunt. She's our realtor. You just see her
so much you started calling her Aunt Carol.

Why didn't we buy her pink house?
It wasn't her house. She was just showing it to us.

Why didn't we buy it?
Daddy doesn't want a pink house.

Oh, Aunt Carol has blonde hair like me!
Yes, she does.

What color eyes does she have?
I don't know.

Who bought the pink house?
I don't know.

What were their names?
I don't know.

Why not?
I DON'T KNOW!!!

MESSING WITH MY SYSTEM

My days have been extremely busy, which I actually enjoy most of the time. I have been going nonstop from the time I wake up until the time I go to bed. (I am sure this sounds absolutely normal to all of you out there.) I have been waking up very early every morning raring to go.

However, this morning I woke up at 6:15 and then fell back asleep. I woke up again at 7:20, startled, thinking Max was going to be late for school. I jumped out of bed and found Seth and Max in the bathroom brushing Max's teeth.

I have a system, which usually includes picking out Max and Ella's outfits the night before. I found that Seth had dressed Max. Uh oh, not that!

"I didn't pick out his outfit," I stutter. "Rebecca, I found him clothes. Everything is okay. I wanted you to sleep. You slept through my alarm and I figured you must be really tired."

I know you are all thinking, "What a wonderful husband." You are all thinking, "Just say thank you." Nope, I keep going. "I wanted to pick out his outfit and I wanted to pack his lunch!" I am literally twitching while I say this to Seth. I should be saying "Thank you." Sorry, Seth!

You see, when I went to sleep last night, I figured out what I wanted Max to wear. Yes, I am this anal! I also pack Max's lunch the night before. I get everything ready and then I have a system as to how it gets packed.

Max has a special lunchbox that has built-in freezer packs. He saw the commercial on TV before kindergarten started last year, and he had to have it. It actually works really well. The lunch box is called a "pack it" if you want to look it up.

Okay, so back to my insanity. Max picked out a stainless steel Star Wars water bottle that I pack every day with his food, a napkin, a note, and hand sanitizer. One of the best tips I have gotten from a parent was to pack the hand sanitizer so Max can eat lunch with clean hands. I rip open Max's backpack, rip open the lunchbox, and panic that Seth forgot to pack Max's water. "You forgot the water bottle. He needs a drink," I say to Seth, who tells me, "He would be okay without a drink Rebecca." My husband is really good at mellowing me out. I am way too uptight!

Seth is annoyed at this point. I don't blame him. I get nervous when he actually uses my name, instead of "honey" or "sweetie."

How does Seth think Max would be okay without a drink? I can hear it now, "Mom, you didn't pack my drink! I had to tell the lunch lady and they had to have me get some milk because you forgot my water!"

You see, Seth isn't home when Max gets home, and he doesn't have to deal with how Max's day has gone. I realize having to drink milk is not a big deal, but I want my boy to have his water bottle.

Seth doesn't get it. He doesn't get his anal, organized, neat-freak wife. He also doesn't get how much I have chilled out since I met him, and how insanely neat I really am.

You see, I try hard for Seth not to be as anal as I really want to be. I look at how he puts things away and I still cringe. I see how he "fixes" things and I get angry at his "half ass" attempt. The bottom line is I wish I was more like Seth. Don't fall over anyone!

I need to loosen up. I need to not panic over what Max is wearing and if Seth remembered to pack everything in his lunch. None of this is a big deal.

If we want our husbands to help us shouldn't we be praising them?

"Thank you honey for picking out Max's outfit," (even though I would never pick that). "Thank you, sweetheart for packing Max's lunch," (even though you forgot his water). "Thank you honey for brushing his teeth," (even though there is now toothpaste everywhere that I will now compulsively clean up). "Thank you, my love for fixing the drawer in the fridge," (even though you didn't actually fix it).

Oh women, do we ever learn? How about just, "Thank you."

Thank you, my husband for being so amazing. I love you Seth

more than my words could ever tell you. I will work on just saying thank you for all the wonderful things you do every day! I truly appreciate you Seth.

ACTIVITIES

Activities have always been a battle in my house. How does that make any sense?

I see my friends' children popping around to baseball, soccer, ice skating, swimming, tennis, martial arts, gymnastics, dance, hockey, religion. You name it, my friends' children are doing it. Isn't that normal? Isn't that what kids do? They go to school and they have activities to do.

When I was younger my mom would let my brother and I do one activity at a time, so she wasn't running all over creation driving us everywhere. Smart lady! My kids have a mother who will drive all over creation. They don't know how good they have it? Does any kid?

I have forced it along for many years now. I forced Max to try T-ball and he and Seth hated it, complaining to me that it was boring.

I attempted to put Max in Hebrew school as a kindergartener and he cried and cried for many reasons I could go on and on about.

I put him in soccer and forced him to go every week. I watched Max whiz along the field loving every minute of playing, and yet the following week it was a battle again.

I put him in swimming and tennis over the summers and drag him kicking and screaming while he wailed that he wants to stay home and do nothing, and then watched him love swimming and love playing tennis. My child makes no logical sense to me!

I dragged him to Tae Kwon Do two to three days a week for eight months. He continued to tell me he'd had enough and was ready to try something else. It was so good for him. It helped him focus. It gave him flexibility and strength. I loved his instructor. I loved what he was learning. How long was I going to force it?

Where is the commitment, the passion, the drive? He wants to be home. He wants to play with his friends. I know, I know, he is only six!

I listen to Ella tell me all summer she can't wait to take dancing. I sign her up for dancing and we head off to the studio, where I've chosen her preschool music teacher to be her dancing teacher. Guess what? She hides behind me telling me she is too nervous and won't go in. I hear a girl crying in the room and wonder how her mom so easily left her. I just can't do it.

Ella is now begging for gymnastics. Seriously kid! What happened to dance? "Come on child of mine!"

I drag Max to Hebrew school today (now first grade) talking it up, explaining how much fun he is going to have and how much he is going to learn. I also begin telling him he needs to pick one activity to do other than Hebrew school. We survived through day one of Hebrew school! Point for mama! Point for Max!

I look in front of me at Temple at all the teenagers sitting there ready to volunteer their time at Hebrew school. My mind starts traveling to my kids being teenagers and needing to be good students, good athletes, good musicians, and do great volunteer work. They need to be well-rounded so they get into college. Whoa mama! Snap back to 2013! Your kiddos are six, four, and almost one. All is okay. Let's stay in the present moment and not go spiraling to 10 years later!

Both kids are registered for Hebrew school. Both kids are asking for gymnastics. "Max, you are awesome at soccer. Let's do soccer again." "No Mom, I want to do gymnastics. I keep telling you I really want to do gymnastics." Hebrew school and gymnastics. Should be interesting!

It is a day of realizations. My kids are only six and four. They really don't need to be doing any activities. They have plenty of time to get involved.

I will get them involved. I will do my best to help them find their passions in life. I will find that middle ground. I don't want to be the drill sergeant parent forcing my kids to excel at something they don't want to do. I also don't want to be the pushover parent who lets them quit everything they try.

Whether they want to be gymnasts, painters or singers, I will be the cheerleader parent cheering my kids on in whatever they choose.

I wrote this almost seven years ago. Fast forward to my editing this today on November 15, 2019. I am laughing at myself and my concern over Max and Ella at ages 6 and 4. I was expecting them to have passion at a very early age. That is very funny! Today Max is turning 13 soon and is a passionate, talented soccer goalie. Ella is a passionate actress, dancer and singer. Lillie seems to love dancing, and I see cheerleading in her future. We want our kids to do pro-social activities, it is good for them for so many reasons. I wish I could have talked to myself years ago and told myself to relax. It is good to see that I am learning and growing. I hope all your children are finding activities that they enjoy!

THE SECRET DECODER RING
BY SETH GREENE

Women complain all the time about the fact that men don't understand them.

I have the secret decoder ring.

When she says "I have too much to do" she really means, "Go do some of it and don't ask me any annoying questions. Just help the way I want you to without me telling you what that is."

When she says, "I don't like this house," she really means "Go work your ass off and buy me a new house."

When she says "These kids drive me nuts," she really means "Take them with you out of the house somewhere and give me a break – but instead of sitting and relaxing for once in my life I'm really going to clean the house because I just can't help myself."

I think part of the reason men don't really understand women is that women don't understand themselves.

SECRET SUCCESS SCHOOL
BY SETH GREENE

So, Ella started UPK this year, and loves it.

She is now obsessed with playing pre-school when she gets home, and she gets to be the teacher. I have tried to involve Max in this, but he says, "I'm in first grade, this is too babyish for me."

Then he tells me, "Daddy, I had a dream that when I grow up, I'm going to be as successful as you and make as much money as you do. I really hope it comes true."

I tear up, hug him, and tell him, "What you have learned about business and marketing at age six, took me until age 30 to learn. You're going to be way more successful than me." "You really think so, Daddy?" "I know so. What if we started a secret success school?"

He leans in, eyes wide, looks around and whispers, "What's secret success school?" And I know I've got him.

I go to the kiddie white board Ella uses and draw a triangle. "Ella what's this?" Ella can't take the suspense. She's jumping up and down. "A triangle Daddy. I love secret success school!"

"Do you know what this triangle represents, Max?" He's not sure what I'm looking for. "This is the secret to success." "How?" I write one word on each point of the triangle.

"What is this word?" "Market." "Market is who you sell your products to. If we try to promote your Skylander affiliate videos to people who don't have the $14 to buy a Skylander, is that a good market?" "No, I won't make any sales." G-d do I love him, he's getting it at six.

"Hey, I have enough money in my wallet to buy a Skylander Swap Force right now! If I keep making more money, I can get lots of them!" –That's how you inspire a work ethic.

"What's the next word Max?" "M-M-Media? What's that?" "How you tell your customers to buy. How do you get in front of your customers? Do you sell them via a book?" "No Daddy. It's online. It's at Whinypaluza.com."

"I am so proud of you. How do we tell them about the website?" "Facebook! Like what Mommy does on her phone."

"What's the next word?"
"Message, " he replies. "That's why they should buy from you," I teach.
"Because I'm a kid, and I love Skylanders, and I know which ones are good and which ones are lame!" he answers.
 "I'm not sure I would use the word lame, but YES! That's exactly it! The better you put those three words together the more money you will make."
"I can do that Daddy!"

Now I have to figure out what to do next, because I know he's going to ask for the next class when I get home.

PREGNANCY NUMBER THREE

We had our son Max and our daughter Ella. Life was starting to get a little easier, and Ella was out of diapers. We could both taste the freedom.

Seth kept telling me he was done and didn't want any more children. Seth would say "I got my boy, I got my girl, and I am good!"

I begged and pleaded for just one more baby and Seth kept telling me he was good. "I will win this one," I would tease my husband.

Seth continued to say no and attempted to convince me in his salesman way that we were good with two children. "I am trying to protect you. You don't need more work and we need more time together." I would ignore Seth and tell him I wanted my May baby.

"You don't understand, Ella needs a sister. Have you seen how close sisters are? I haven't had an uneventful birth, I'm due for one!" I would plead my case to Seth. He took a new route, which was, "We will talk about it in September," knowing that would give me the May baby I always wanted. Now he knew he was at least off the hook until then!

Seth did a great job in those next several months convincing me we were good with two kids. I started to drop the subject.

I started to hear his points. I was listening and I was now debating whether my husband was right. Could he possibly have good points?

We are driving home one night, and I tell Seth he has to stop and buy me some Nerd candies. I literally had to have them and begged him to get me some. I have never in my life asked for Nerds. Seth looked at me like I was crazy and stopped at CVS. He came out with Nerds and a pregnancy test!

I am totally freaked out! A positive pregnancy test, how could this be? I'm thinking "Seth is going to be so upset," as I scream from the bathroom!

Seth walks in, looks at the test, and is all smiles! "You are happy?" I ask my husband, totally confused. He was thrilled and felt like this was meant to be. Phew!

Seth was the pregnancy police for the next nine months. He wanted me to take it easy, and there was no messing with him! The bigger I got, the less he let me do. He was cooking, shopping, taking care of the kids, working, taking the kids all over the place and somehow staying sane.

They would leave to go to the zoo, and I would cry. Seth would remind me that three kids would be crazy, and I would be busier than imaginable before I knew it. "I will chain you to the recliner," Seth would threaten me. He was willing to do what it took to avoid the NICU again. My hero! My Superman! Mr. Mom!

I did more praying than I probably ever have. My son was an emergency C-section and my daughter was six weeks early and sent to the NICU. I was ready for an uneventful birth. I kept saying "The third time is the charm!"

I went to the hospital a couple times totally freaked out that I was in labor, but I was happily wrong both times. This time when my water broke, my baby was ready, and she was full term! 37 weeks! I made it! We made it!

Off to the hospital we go. (Why is it always the middle of the night by the way?) The prep was easy, the C-section was easy and guess what...the recovery was easy! I felt great and I was ready to go home with my Lillie Rose! Lillie, thank you for giving me that uneventful birth that I always dreamed of. Seth, thank you for making me lie on the recliner. A sister for Ella! I get to see what sisters are like. I know what you are all thinking. What about Max? Yes, Max wants a brother, but you know what I have to say about that? Max will love being a big brother to two sisters! You know what Seth has to say? Shop is closed! Three is our number! Our party of five is complete!

COMMUNICATION
BY SETH GREENE

How men and women communicate. You be the judge.

Rebecca:
You were home with the girls today, what did you do?
Seth:
I took the girls to Build-A-Bear. Ella built a Smurf. We walked around the mall for a little bit and ate Mrs. Fields cookies. We came home.

Four sentences. Less than 30 seconds.

Now let's see Rebecca's take – doing exactly the same thing (literally, just a different day).

Rebecca:
Having three kids means it can be difficult to spend quality time with each child. Max loves to go to the movies with me so we have had several Mommy-Max movie dates. Ella was complaining that she wanted an Ella-Mommy Build-A-Bear date. My girlfriend was taking her daughter to a My Little Pony Party at Build-A-Bear, which I thought would be perfect for Ella. Ella loves My Little Pony and she was even going to get to make a stuffed My Little Pony at the party. Ella was so excited, and she was debating which pony she would get to make.

We show up at the party and Ella is jumping up and down and can't wait to go in and choose a pony. The ponies are both so pretty and I am so excited for my baby. It is so interesting as an adult how much fun I still have seeing my daughter do things that I know I would have loved as a child. I take Max to the toy store and I find myself drifting down the girl aisles wanting to pick out stuff for Ella. Ella has a dollhouse, a kitchen, a Barbie dollhouse, a Barbie car, over 40 Barbies. She has gotten almost everything I wanted as a child. It is so fun for me! My husband isn't so amused by this.

I can't wait to see which beautiful pony Ella chooses. We walk into Build-A-Bear and Ella starts looking at all her options. "Why are you looking around?" I ask my daughter very confused. "I have to see what all the choices are," Ella is now telling me as she looks at every single stuffed option there is. "I thought you were making a pony for the My Little Pony party," I ask Ella, puzzled by her now lack of interest in making a pony. "Smurfette!" Ella declares. "You want to make Smurfette?" I am beyond confused because she didn't even like the Smurf movie. When we came here last year, I wanted her to make Smurfette because I loved Smurfette as a child, but Ella refused and ended up making Hello Kitty. Now that we are at a My Little Pony party, she chooses Smurfette. I just can't keep up with my child. I should be celebrating that she has a mind of her own. However, I am concerned with the aftermath.

"Ella, you were dying to make a pony. Will you please choose a pony? Mommy doesn't want you to get upset later that you didn't make a pony." I am trying to cover my bases and avoid a tantrum later. "Mommy, I want to make Smurfette. I am not changing my mind. I am not making a pony. I promise I won't get upset later. I just love Smurfette!" "Ella, this is a My Little Pony party. Are you absolutely 100% positive you want to make Smurfette, and that you are still going to be happy with your choice when we leave?" I know my daughter. I know that in a couple hours she is going to want a pony. "No, no, no! I am making Smurfette. I don't want a pony. Just let me make Smurfette!" The women who work at Build-A-Bear are watching this whole scene laughing at the situation. They appear to completely understand what I am going through. My friend is also laughing at my daughter choosing Smurfette. You see, her daughter picked Twilight, and an outfit for Twilight, and even some hair extensions for Twilight the pony. I look around the room. Every single girl is standing there with their new pony. I just have to laugh!

So, I let Ella pick Smurfette against my better judgement. She chooses a dress for Smurfette and she is thrilled. I would say it is now two months after this whole event and Ella is still in love with Smurfette. She plays with Smurfette all the time and carries her all over the place. Her father has also taken her back to Build-A-Bear to get another Smurf. I guess I was wrong. There not only was no pony meltdown, there has also been no request to go get a pony. Go figure! I am very happy to be wrong.

Seth: Here's the funnier part. She knows it!

When I get home, if she has enough energy left over that our little vampires (children) didn't suck out of her, and if the headache they have given her isn't too bad – she will ask how my day was. I will say fine. If she's really in a good mood she might ask for a few more details and get a few sentences out of me.

Here is her knowing about how she communicates:
When I get home she says, "Let me tell you about my day." I will urge her to just give me the end result. She will say, "I will but let me tell you what happened first." "I don't need the whole story." "I know and I will try and be quick."

End result – she went to Reeds Jewelers to buy some Alex & Ani bracelets – her new obsession. She bought two for herself and gave two to her friend. Two sentences. It took her about five minutes to tell me the "quick version" of that story.

My wife will go out to dinner with her friends, and will have been there for two hours, and I will text her and she will tell me they haven't even ordered yet!

Rebecca's response:
Okay, so in my defense Seth, I told you about all my errands and ALL the money I spent! I also told you all the people I bumped into. I know you love me! You didn't want to marry a man. Women give details. This is why women love talking to women! I love you honey.

CRAZY SEPTEMBER

Oh September, I wish you a happy farewell. You are always crazy, and this year we decided to make it even crazier!

Nine years ago, when my mother suggested Labor Day weekend for a wedding, I cringed. I wanted May, and I was never a September fan. However, Seth and my mom won, and I went along with them. It really was a great idea. I now get to end summer and begin the school year celebrating one of the most wonderful days of my life. Don't throw up, it is true.

Let's move on to the start of school. My kids had an amazing summer, as usual. Swimming, tennis, dancing, friends, sleeping in, hours and hours in my parents' pool. They had it made! So, Max and Ella are both on the floor crying that they didn't want to go back to school. Tough! School is your job for the next long while, so get used to it!

School supplies
Back packs
Clothes
Lunches
Schedules
Bedtimes
Homework

Yes, I was dreading it too. We have all managed to get back into the groove of things. Ella is loving preschool, and I am loving how easy it feels with only one child. How is it that when I had Max, I thought one child was hard?

Max is another story. He is not so thrilled with first grade. What is with all the homework? He is six! The education department has gotten totally messed up, yes, I said messed up, with what they expect of very young children. Give them more recess time. Give them a ball. Let them play, people! Can you tell I am NOT HAPPY? I am that mom. The mom that wants the teacher to focus on teaching my six-year-old to love school. Teach him a love for education; don't shove it down his throat. This gets me so fired up!

Anniversary, check.
Started school, check.

Now there are three, yes THREE Jewish holidays to celebrate in September. Rosh Hashanah, Yom Kippur and Sukkot. Let's throw in Lillie's naming with Sukkot and make even more work for Mommy! Yes me, the one who asks for more stuff to do every day. Women just say NO! Let's work on teaching our daughters this please, because we were taught to say YES!

We celebrate Rosh Hashanah and we observe Yom Kippur. I drag my kids to Temple. My kids are going to learn to love their religion! They have it made. Their services are fun. They even had a puppet show during their service. Back in my day, we walked up a hill to Temple through the rain and the snow and...just kidding! Back in my day the services were just not as fun as they are now. My kids, as usual, have NO IDEA how good they have it!

Two holidays down, now on to Sukkot! The Temple puts a Sukkah in my backyard, and we celebrate by having the Rabbi bless the Sukkah and bless Lillie at the same time with her Hebrew name! Fabulous idea! It was wonderful! I forgot to mention that in the midst of all of this I was getting our house ready to go on the market!

Anniversary, Check.
Started school, Check.
Three holidays and a naming, Check.
Buy a house, Check!
Get your house on the market so you can sell it quickly! Did I give myself enough stuff to do in September?

House is cleaned, house is organized, house is on the market. Thank heavens my house sold in one day! I don't think this mama could have handled showings for more than one day!

House sold, Check!
House inspected, Check!
September is over, CHECK!!!

Goodbye September. Let's hope October is a little slower!
We will start it with my daughter's first birthday. There are a bunch of birthdays. I need to pack up my house. Who are we kidding? October is going to be crazy too! I think I just tell myself that each month is going to be less crazy to help myself cope with the current crazy! Bring on October!

WALMART II
BY SETH GREENE

Rebecca decided that today should be the day Max gets a new bike.

My thought is, "It's Fall and he doesn't have that long to ride it, and next spring he will have grown – (because she keeps feeding him even though I tell her to cut that out) but what the heck, let's go get it anyway."

Yesterday Lillie broke her Binkie string, so we have to go get a new one of those. Ella's Smurfette Halloween costume is too small, so we need to go find one in the right size. Walmart will probably be the cheapest option, so let's go there.

Apparently, my lovely wife doesn't read her own blog. She wrote a hilarious column on how painful shopping at Walmart with kids can be. The pain from that trip has faded from her memory, so off we go.

Plus, Lillie and Ella didn't let her sleep last night, so she's not in the most resourceful state to begin with. This should be fun.

We get to Walmart and the fun begins.

Max wants to look at the bikes first. Ella wants to look at more Barbies (even though that's not why we are here).

We go look at bikes. We think Max needs a 20″ bike. He tries to ride one. It's too big. He thinks that means he just needs to keep trying other 20″ bikes until he finds the magic one that fits.

I try to explain that he needs the next size down. He tries an 18″ and it fits. He doesn't like the color. It turns out that Walmart only has one (that's right one) 18″ in the whole store.

My naïve, optimistic wife says, "Maybe they have more in the back." It takes me seven minutes to go find an actual employee. Of course, he doesn't work in bikes, but he will go find a manager. He disappears into the Bermuda triangle, never to return.

We give up. Max is all upset. To distract him, we go look at toys. Max discovers that Bey Blades has come out with new Bey Figures. Same toy concept – but it's an action figure on top of the spinning top. He has to have one. He decides to spend his own money on one. Woohoo, I'm off the hook.

We look at girl toys, and Ella wants us to buy every baby toy for Lillie. So sweet. Except lately, she and Max seem to have more fun with Lillie's toys than Lillie does. If only I knew then what I know now.

I find my wife shopping for a birthday present for Ella's friend who loves horses. Rebecca is checking out any horse she sees and asking Ella about it. Seriously people, that wasn't on the list she gave me.

This is another issue. Rebecca tells me what we are going to a store for. I then treat it like a military operation. I want to get to those items in as direct a route as we can. No distractions. No stopping anywhere else. Get the items and proceed to the extraction point.

Being in a store makes Rebecca remember all the other stuff she's been thinking about buying, but never told me about. This does not make for a very harmonious trip.

I really need to loosen up.

The really scary part was after Lillie was born. You see, Ella was born prematurely, so with Lillie I was paranoid. I wouldn't let Rebecca off the couch while she was pregnant, and after she delivered and came home, she was recovering from her third C-section so I wouldn't let her do much then either (other than take care of Lillie). So, it was probably a good six months since she had been in a store.

The first time she went shopping by herself I got a call from our credit card company. "Mr. Greene? It's MasterCard. We noticed some suspicious activity on your card today and wanted to call you before we processed the transaction." That was an interesting dinner table conversation when I got home.

Sending Rebecca into any store can be scary because she finds multiple things we "need" but that weren't on her list.

Next, we go to get milk. This should be simple, but it's not. Rebecca is working on weaning Lillie from breast feeding and wants to start giving her some milk.

What kind of milk? Almond milk doesn't have enough fat in it. Oops, that's lite almond milk. Let's try regular. Nope. Not enough fat.

"Lillie at 12 months almost weighs more than Ella at 4½ years old. Maybe we don't need much fat?" I really should work on keeping my mouth shut about this stuff.

Apparently, I don't know anything about babies, what a surprise. It turns out that babies need fat for brain development, my wife tells me. You see, while I am reading tons of stuff about growing my businesses my wife is reading about baby and kid stuff.

Then we try rice milk. Nope, that doesn't work either. What about regular whole cow's milk? That has lots of fat, except my in-laws own a health food store and they would go completely meshuggenah on us if we let their granddaughter drink actual cow's milk. Rebecca goes with both almond and rice milk, and we will try both and see how they go.

By this time Lillie has gotten hungry. Maybe it was looking at all that milk. Here is where my wife absolutely amazes me. I may be a magician, but I have no freaking clue how she does this trick.

She holds Lillie in one arm. She holds a squeezable packet of organic baby food in the other. She then manages to squeeze the packet one slurp at a time into Lillie's mouth, without spilling one drop.

Did I mention she is also walking, yelling at Max & Ella, telling me what to do, and shopping at the same time? Seriously people, this goes way beyond walking and chewing gum. When I try feeding Lillie right from the packet (as opposed to putting it into a bowl and using a spoon), I make a huge mess, and Rebecca usually has to change Lillie's entire outfit.

Then Rebecca notices that Lillie is missing a sock. She hands Lillie to me, tells me to feed her and keep the other two kids in line, while she goes back through the whole store – retracing our steps to find the missing sock.

Seriously? Can't I just give you $1.99 for new socks and save the time, stress, and aggravation? I guess not.

I cannot hold Lillie and feed her. I know my limits. I stick her in the cart and feed her, and still manage to make a mess. Max & Ella keep running in and out of the clothes section, playing hide and go seek. I try not to yell too loudly.

They keep asking when Mommy is coming back, and why did she leave again? Max says, "Maybe the sock fell out in the cart." "No way Max. Then mommy would be wandering all over the store, stressed out for nothing. She'd be really mad."

"But what if Daddy? Maybe you should look." I look. The kid is right! The sock fell out in the cart. He could have said something five minutes ago.

I pray that Rebecca has her phone with her. I text her the good news. She doesn't respond. Uh oh. This isn't looking good people. I start thinking of excuses I can make when she gets back. Maybe Ella will have to go pee all of a sudden and get me out of this.

Rebecca comes back on her own (never got my text). She doesn't look happy as she couldn't find the sock. I show her the sock. You can insert your own string of expletives here. Let your imagination run wild, you won't be far off.

The good news is she managed to find a birthday present on her search around the store which did seem to distract her from her aggravation about the sock.

Next, we go look at costumes. Ella finds the Disney princess costumes and wants them all. I remind her that she already OWNS them ALL. She has Rapunzel, Cinderella, Belle, Ariel, etc.

"Okay Daddy." Thank G-d.

However, they do not have Smurfette. Now she's all upset. "I'm never going to get to be Smurfette, Daddy! What am I going to do?"

Dear Lord, when does it end? Rebecca promises Ella to find a Smurfette costume that fits her and Ella calms down.

Max is looking at the boy costumes. Rebecca already bought Max's costume. He is going to be the Skylander Giant Crusher. Thank G-d the costume doesn't come with Crusher's giant sledgehammer.

"Look Daddy, a bow and arrow guy!" (Robin Hood). "Look Daddy, a ninja!" (He was a ninja last year) "Max, we're not here to look at costumes for you, you already have yours." "But Daddy–" "–No More Buts! Let's go!" "Daddy you said buts." "Ok Beavis, let's go. Your mother's exhausted." "Who's Beavis?" "Never mind."

Finally, thank the Lord, we got out of Walmart alive. Now on to Toy-R-Us.

Rebecca once again swears she will never go back to Walmart. I will keep you posted on that one!

THE PUMPKIN PATCH

"You will go to the Pumpkin Patch and you will have a good time!" I yell at my son who is now telling me he doesn't want to go to the Pumpkin Patch because his friends are outside playing.

I tell my pouting son, "You can play with them when we get home! Rides, games, animals, pumpkins, junk food….seriously you should be begging me to go!"

I get the kids all ready to go and by this time I am profusely sweating. Why did I take a shower? What is the point? I have the diaper bag, the jackets, a binkie, a stroller. I think I am good.

I walk inside to grab Lillie and Seth thinks he is funny. "Lillie pooped," he yells. He'd better change her. I am running around like a crazy person. He can help me and change the darn poop!

He is already on his way to change Lillie before I even utter a word. You see Seth knows HOW HARD it is for me to get out of the house, so he really does his best to help.

Phew! We are all in the car and ready to go! It ALWAYS feels like such a great accomplishment. I give myself a mental pat on the back every time I get out of the house.

Lillie at one years old still hates the car. Unless she is asleep, she tends to be complaining to get out of the car. I decide to start singing "the wheels on the bus," and we all sing to Lillie. It actually works and Lillie is now giggling instead of crying!

Seth pays for our admission, and in we go. We have to go through the Pumpkin Patch store to get to the Patch. This is not very helpful Pumpkin People. Thanks a lot!

Now Max is screaming to buy him this and that in the Pumpkin Patch store. Seth keeps saying, "We can buy it on the way out." As if he's really going to be in the mood to spend any more money on the way out.

I drag Max out of the store and he starts screaming to see all the animals. "Don't touch anything!" I am feeling my germ phobia kick in as I watch my kids head to touch all the dirty farm animals. "You are such an indoor girl," My husband declares. "Excuse me?" Wrong thing to say to this summer worshipper.

I cringe but I let the kids feed the animals. Yuck!
We head straight to the hand sanitizer and then we are off to get them a snack. Yes, they want to eat already. Are you surprised?

This one wants popcorn, then this one wants frozen chocolate covered cheesecake on a stick, then this one wants lemonade. "For the love of G-d, slow down so I can get one thing at a time."

Seth saves the table for us but appears to be spending all his time trying to swat bees with the admission program. The cheesecake was a big hit by the way. We passed it around to all of us and Lillie looked in awe of what she was eating. My head is spinning but we make it through snacks and defending ourselves from lots of bees!

It is October but it is an unseasonably hot day and we are all sweating. I dressed us all totally wrong, so we are all over-heated.

Here I thought it would be a great day to go. It is nice out and the Buffalo Bills are playing so lots of people will be watching football. Wrong! The place is packed, and Seth is giving me that look of "how much longer do I have to suffer?" We haven't even been here that long!

The kids pass the face painting deciding the line is way too long. Phew! Got out of waiting in that long line!

They want to go on a hayride. We think it's right next to us, but it turns out it's not the hayride, that's the wagon ride. Are they kidding me? We learned that the wagon ride costs extra money, but the hayride doesn't. These people are unreal.

We now have more walking to do to get to the hayride. Seth is not happy. Neither is Lillie, and I can't decide if Lillie is going to make it through a hayride. We walk and walk and walk until we find the line. Another long line, oh joy! What are all these people doing in my line? Don't they have better things to do?

The kids have no patience and they don't want to wait in this line either. Ella tells us she wants to go on a tiny short hayride. I explain that once she gets on, she has to stay on till the end, and she wants nothing to do with it. Well, let's look at the bright side. I am certainly getting some exercise walking all over this place.

Max now sees the pumpkin launcher and he is off to launch pumpkins. This was a hit! Ella cheered Max on, and Lillie giggled the whole time. As a bonus, the line was short!

Games, rides, playground, at this point Seth and I are wondering if this will ever end. We both LOVE taking our children to do fun things and yet we find ourselves overstimulated.

Max and Ella decide to play some games and waste our money. This always drives Seth nuts. You see, in his non-existent spare time he is a professional magician. So, he never shuts up about how each game is rigged so you can't really win.

Don't even get him started on how we have to waste $6 in games to win a toy we could get from Oriental Trading for 50 cents (but he never seems to actually buy the kids any of the toys. He just likes to bitch about it). He does this at every carnival, so I have just gotten in the habit of tuning him out.

I see how much fun they have, so I keep handing out money for more games to win more stuff that we don't need. I see

Seth's face begin to change shades of red. I see the warning signs. Daddy is going to blow people!

"Let's stop playing games and move on to something else," I tell my kids as I begin dragging them away. Okay, crisis averted. I stopped the children from playing crappy games and winning crappy stuff that I end up throwing away anyway.

More drinks, more snacks. Are they kidding me? Didn't we JUST feed them?

We head to the bakery and look around. The kids are staring at all the candy. Somehow, we made it out with little lollipops for each of them. That was not an easy task!

Max and Ella are now screaming for pumpkins. We settle for some pictures in front of the pumpkins. Max is trying to hold Lillie in the pictures and Lillie is screaming. The kids aren't smiling in any of  the pictures but by this point who cares!

"We want to buy pumpkins," Max and Ella are chanting to us. "We have pumpkins," I remind them. Apparently, our pumpkins aren't good enough because they are from the grocery store.

Seth declares "Let's go!" I drag them kicking and screaming because we didn't get to the playground or rides. "Another day!" Seth and I say in unison.

I am eyeing all the beautiful mums as we walk out but I don't dare say a word about buying any. I remember there is a beautiful pumpkin stake I wanted to buy in the store, but I keep my mouth shut. I see the exit and I am almost home free. Do not stop, do not stop, head straight to the car!

The kids are in the car. The stroller is in the car. We did it. We exited the Pumpkin Patch. Once again, I find myself giving myself a mental pat on the back for getting us all back in the car. Amazing what an accomplishment that always feels like to me on a daily basis.

I look at Seth "Wasn't that fun?" I ask. "A ball," Seth sarcastically says as he heads for home. Another adventure in the books!

MONOPOLY
BY SETH GREENE

Lately, Max has become obsessed with playing Monopoly. Disney Junior Monopoly, Monopoly Millionaire, Skylanders Monopoly, original Monopoly...he likes them all.

Max and Ella play very differently.

Max plays to win. He trash talks. He does a little dance when you land on his properties. He buys everything he lands on (I'm working with him on that). He overpays during an auction. Max wants to play the long version and play till the very end.

We played at my dad's house on Christmas. My dad got him the Skylanders version of Monopoly – combining two of Max's favorite things.

My dad purposely (I think) made a bad trade so the game would end sooner. Max figured out it was a trade that made no sense if Gramps was really trying to win and asked me later if we could have a rematch. We did, just Max and me. I won, but it was close.

Ella could not be more different. She has played the real version three times. The first two times she lasted five minutes and then went back to playing with her Barbies. Tonight, was the first time she played the entire game.

I couldn't stop laughing. I tried to help her. She bought properties because she liked the color. She thinks it's more fun to put properties up for auction then to just buy them. She would randomly offer to give Max money. "No honey, that's not the point of the game." "But I want to help him. He wants more money, and I want him to have it." "Keep your money and sit down Ella."

Twice she bought a property that he needed to complete a monopoly. I thought she was getting it. Then she tried to give it to Max. Max was very excited about this, "Yeah, Ella, give me the monopoly and then you are going to lose." Picture him standing on his chair doing his butt dance while he sings this.

"Ella don't give him that. He needs it, and he has no properties to trade that will help you. Keep it and you can stop him from getting that monopoly." "But I want to give it to him. When I bought it he was so upset and when I said I would give it to him he started dancing." "But he will win. You are supposed to be trying to win."

"Oh. Can I change my playing token for my Smurfette doll? Smurfette would like to land on the pretty purple properties." "Sure, Ella, go get Smurfette." I give up.

Mommy's take:
Today, instead of folding the laundry, I decided to join in the Monopoly fun that has been going on around me. "Hey," I say to Seth, "I want to play too. I don't want to do work. I want to play!"

Seth was happily surprised, and I started smiling remembering the many games of Monopoly I played with my brother growing up. Seth warned me that Max plays like him and Ella plays like me. This should be interesting!

I am giggling as I watch my daughter shout "auction" turn after turn. Ella has no interest in buying properties and Max wants every single one. He starts bidding against Seth and me and wins the auction. He realizes he doesn't have the $300 to cover his bill.

I then start organizing his money so he can see what he has. Seth starts laughing and then watches me start to organize his properties. "Why are you organizing my properties? You just can't help yourself!"

Max is getting upset that he doesn't have money and he rolls snake eyes (a pair of ones). Trying to help him out, I ask Seth to give Max one of each bill for getting snake eyes, but my stickler husband tells me it isn't in the rules.

Max now draws a card that makes him have to pay each of us $50. I tell him not to worry about it. Seth is beginning to see that he doesn't want me in on these Monopoly games. I land on one of Max's properties and tell him I want to give him a tip. Seth is not amused.

I now have a monopoly (oops how did I do that) and Seth wants me to put up houses. Not yet.

Max is now very upset that he can't buy any properties, and he wants a monopoly, so I throw one of my properties at him. Seth gives it back to me and tells me I can't do that. Seth is no fun!

Now I'm thinking I should buy some houses. I then land on free parking and they throw more money at me. I try to give Max a $100 bill and Seth gives it back. Man is he tough.

I now decide that since I have more money, I will put more houses on my monopoly. Max gets more upset. He is ready to blow. I just want Seth to give him the property he wants, but he is being a good dad and is trying to teach Max about business. He is trying to do a trade with him, but I am not liking this trade. "You are cheating your son!" Seth says, "I am not cheating I am teaching him about supply and demand."

Ella is just continuing to yell "auction" during the game and is becoming bored. She has gone from my lap to now wandering into the playroom to play. Lillie is now up from her nap, and Max is now storming off from the table because he thinks he is losing.

"Welcome to Monopoly chaos," Seth laughs. That was fun! Now Ella is begging Max to come back to the game, and I am off to the kitchen to make Lillie lunch. I have a feeling Seth is not going to want me to play the next game.

MOVING

I have been very busy moving my family to a new home. Life has been completely crazy!

It took me about six months to pack up my house. I just kept asking, "How much stuff do we have?" We lived in a 1,900 square foot ranch, and I just couldn't figure out where I was keeping all this stuff! I had no idea how hard it would be to pack up while parenting three children. That was a challenge for sure.

People kept telling me, "Hire, hire, hire." Who are we kidding? Have you figured out yet that I am a control freak? I wanted to pack EVERY box! It drove Seth crazy! "Donate, trash, give to someone, keep." I was making constant piles while I packed. I wasn't about to keep all this stuff we had! (I mean all this very important stuff that we all just had to buy.) I had a system and I didn't want anyone to mess with it!

Seth tried hard to help me. He did pack a ton of boxes. He couldn't understand my limitations of what he could pack. Let's fast forward to unpacking at the new house. As I unpacked the boxes Seth packed, I found a bunch of stuff and would ask him, "Why did you pack this stuff?" The good man that he is, Seth would laugh it off, and tell me I could never have packed every box and he needed to help me!

Moving day completely sucked! The new owners wanted us out by 6 p.m. No way! The movers couldn't even get there until the afternoon. They moved up their deadline to 8:00 the next morning with a request to give them keys around 9 p.m. Let's do this!

When the movers showed up, they seemed amazed by all our stuff. One mover complained the whole day! Aren't we paying him to do this? Why is he complaining?

Thankfully our new house is less than three miles from the old one, so Seth and I were running back and forth with the movers. 9 p.m. on the dot the new owners are calling me. Are you kidding me? Go away! I am scrubbing your floors so let me finish! The wife yells at me and tells me to call her when I am done cleaning. Can I ask you why I sold to this lady? I don't like her at all!

I got desperate and bothered my father at 10 p.m. to please come help us finish so we could get the heck out! We loaded all three of our cars and, "Woohoo, old house is empty! Mission accomplished!"

11 p.m. Seth and I finished unpacking our cars at our new house. My parents gave up and put the kids to bed at their house hours ago. How romantic, Seth and I get to spend our first night in our new house all alone. We collapsed and slept through the night. After seven years of getting up with kids we actually slept through the night! Now that is romance!

So here we are unpacking, unpacking and unpacking. Forget Chanukah, the kids can't believe all the toys that were packed up that they get to play with again. Why did I buy them new toys for Chanukah? I should have wrapped up old toys we had in storage!

The water guy
The cable guy
The furnace guy
The cable guy again
The painters
The cable guy again
The painters again
The handyman

The list goes on and on of people in and out of our new home. It is all coming together!

Ella has named her new pink bedroom Disney World.
Ella has named Max's new green bedroom Sky Land.

Ella has named Lillie's lilac room Owl Land and asked that I give Lillie an owl themed bedroom.

Life in our new house is good as we continue to get settled and enjoy more space. The kids, the cats, Seth and I are adjusting to a new house, new street, new classes, new friends. I am sure there will be a lot more to come to entertain you from my family.

Happy New House!

HOW NOT TO GET YOUR WIFE'S ATTENTION
BY SETH GREENE

How NOT to get your wife's attention:

Go to the same high school but don't talk to her, as she is the captain of the cheerleading team and you consider her way out of your league.

Sleep through the Yom Kippur service you are supposed to attend with your parents.

Feel so guilty (it is the holiday of repentance after all) that you go to the second service, which is for last names ending in K-Z.

Accidentally sit two rows behind your future wife as she is praying to meet a nice Jewish man in temple.

When she goes to the bathroom, follow her out and give her your business card.

Have her accidentally lose your business card in the bottom of her purse for four months.

Get an email from her right after your current relationship just happens to end (as does hers).

Email her and tell her to call you.

Talk every night for hours before your first date.

Pick her up and be charming.

Have the most amazing first date ever, one that lasts 12 hours.

Propose within nine months of dating.

Get married within nine months of being engaged.

Get pregnant within nine months of marriage.

Get pregnant again 17 months later.

When your son is five and your daughter is three and you are finally out of diapers, accidentally have another baby and start all over again.

Then complain about how her life revolves around the kids and you don't get enough attention and see how she reacts.

NEW YEAR'S EVE ADVENTURES

Happy New Year!

We hope you all had a wonderful holiday season. We celebrated eight crazy nights of Chanukah, Christmas and New Year's. Now I am planning my son's 7th birthday party. No break for mama, but that isn't new!

Every year on New Year's Eve we go to our friends' house. It is a long-standing tradition. Last year Seth wanted to take the kids to First Night downtown and I said no. This year he asked again, and I figured I should be a nice wife and head downtown to the madness (I mean fun festivities).

The kids and Seth are excited to go on a new New Year's Eve adventure. It is freezing out and I hold my baby Lillie close to my body and run quickly to the building from the parking lot. We have arrived, let the crazy begin!

 We head into a room with characters and lines to take pictures with all the different characters. Of course my kids want to wait in the lines and Max is upset he can't seem to find Iron Man.

We take the pictures and head to get their faces painted. "Forget it, the line is crazy." I drag them away to the dance room. Ella's favorite song from the movie *Frozen* is playing and the kids boogie and dance through blowing bubbles.

Max now wants to wait in line for the fitness challenges, but I just don't have the patience for long lines! I drag Max into the toddler room, and he humors me and plays with Ella and Lillie for a while.

We decide to head upstairs. The elevator opens and there it is: rides, bounce houses, food, and tons and tons of people! I bring my family over to the stage so I can enjoy watching all the Irish dancers. The kids are hungry of course so we get in the food line. Seth figures they can't screw up pizza (wrong) so orders pizza for himself and Ella. They are out of every chicken dish I ask for and Seth is now upset that there is nothing for me to eat (I am sticking to healthy food). We sit down to eat, and Seth quickly discovers the pizza is gross and soggy! Back he goes to get chicken fingers for the crew. Seth has also found our Rabbi who is there with his wife and kids and a group of friends. We weren't the only fools (I mean good parents) to head downtown to this chaos!

The kids are now screaming for bounce houses. Lillie, our walking toddler, doesn't want to sit in the stroller or be carried so I am chasing her through the building. Lillie is obsessed with the bounce houses and keeps trying to climb in them. There is no way that I am going into a bounce house, so I keep asking my husband to please go bounce with Lillie and take her down all the slides. Lillie doesn't understand what it means to take turns, so she keeps having a fit.

We come to an obstacle course, so I kindly suggest they all go in. Not so kind of me! Max runs through and flies down the slide to my feet. "Max, where is Ella? Please tell me she is with Daddy?" I wait and wait and wait, and more and more people come out who are not Seth, Ella and Lillie, so I start to worry. Finally, I see Seth's face and it is not happy. Ella comes sliding down the slide and then Seth climbs up with Lillie and slides down. He hands me Lillie and then goes to dive back in yelling that he dropped something. He comes back out happy to have found his phone but not so happy with me for sending him into the obstacle course. Seth explains to me that he had to hold Ella and Lillie while ducking and climbing through ropes. He points to the inside of the obstacle course to show me what I sent him into. Oops, sorry honey!

Max is begging over and over to climb the rock wall where the line barely moves. I distract Max with the pogo stick jumper who is jumping over people as I continue to chase Lillie. Seth is seeing the signs. I am sweating, overstimulated and exhausted. We start to drag the kids to the elevator after allowing one more bounce madness, I mean bounce house.

Before we can leave of course Lillie needs her diaper changed and everyone needs to go to the bathroom. You just start to learn as a parent that things that used to take you two minutes now take about 15 minutes – on a good day!

Time to bundle up and walk through the cold to the car. Good times!

We get home and put Ella and Lillie to bed. Max is determined to stay up so Seth, Max and I plop on the couch to get ready for the ball to drop. Max is trying so hard to keep his eyes open. By 11:30, he is out. The ball is about to drop, and I yell to Max and Seth shakes him, but Max is out cold! We give up and Seth carries Max upstairs.

The next morning Max yells at us that he fell asleep! We explain our efforts to wake him, but Max is in tears. Good times! Happy New Year everyone!

ONE NIGHT GETAWAY

Seth's brother is getting married in June. We get an invitation to an engagement party and decide to leave the kids with my parents and fly to the party for one night. Sounds simple right? Oh, how I crack myself up!

A week before the party, Ella comes down with a fever. A couple days later, Seth discovers a hair wrapped so tightly around Lillie's toe that he calls me to come home and help him. I think Seth is crazy, but I rush home. I can't get anything under the hair to cut it off, so I panic and kick Seth and Lillie out the door to urgent care. Seth knows the owner and I figure it will take two minutes. I told you how I crack myself up! 45 minutes later I drag Ella to the car and run to urgent care. (Thankfully Max is with a friend). I run in and throw a fit that Seth and Lillie are still waiting! Yes, watch out, Mama Bear is on the scene and I am shaking with stress and anger as her toe is turning colors.

A doctor comes in, takes a while, and determines that this is a job for the owner who needs to come in. A hair around a toe has led to hours at urgent care!

The owner comes in, they sedate Lillie and get her all prepped and the doctor is able to successfully remove the hair. We don't have to go to Children's Hospital, and Lillie doesn't need surgery. I take a breath of huge relief!

I forgot to mention the huge fit I made at the poor nurse trying to put an IV into Lillie. My baby! How many times were they going to poke my baby? It was just another day as a parent. You never know what crazy stuff will happen? This was a new one for us!

We are home, Lillie is okay, and Ella is feeling better. Two days later, now Lillie has a fever! Good Lord, does it ever end? How am I going to go away? Is winter over? Let the madness end!

Lillie's fever passes and we decide to go to the party. Do you know what this means? There is clean and dirty laundry everywhere. (Sick children make it harder to keep up with crazy insane amounts of laundry that my family makes for me.) I now become laundry superwoman and organize and wash and fold five loads of laundry in order to get organized and pack for all five of us. Seth, I know you did pack for yourself. I am sure it was easier with all the clean organized laundry.

For ONE night I packed clothes, diapers, snacks, movies, a game, stuffed animals, a blanket, binkies, a sippy cup...and that is just for the children! I unloaded about four bags to my parents' house for my kids to do an overnight. I then had to begin packing my own bag.

So here I am, flying to Virginia! Somehow, I made it here. Two fevers, a hurt toe, tons of laundry and packing, but I did it. I am going to go and have a good time!

MAX TURNS SEVEN

Months before my kids' birthdays they start getting off-the-wall excited. The problem is I was so busy moving that I waited too long to book Max's party!

First Max decided he wanted to have it at the roller rink so we could rent out the rink and invite as many kids as he wanted. When we found out it would have to be in February Max said, "No way!" He wanted the party ON his birthday, and he wasn't budging.

I know what you are thinking. Yes, I am the parent. Yes, I am in charge. However, as a parent, you learn to pick your battles. This was not one of those battles I felt was worth fighting. Safety issues I don't budge on, but a birthday party is not so important to me.

After the same issue with the YMCA adventure room we settled on the Niagara Climbing Center. Max and Seth were thrilled to have it there and I was thrilled to finally have something booked. Step one accomplished!

Moving on to the guest list. Why does it seem every step with Max is a big process? Somehow, we make a list and send invitations out.

Max is talking about his birthday every day. He can't think of anything else. Make it stop! The funny thing is my friends start saying, "He has so much. Is there anything he wants?" That just cracks me up because my spoiled children always have a list of stuff they want!

It is now a week before Max's kid party, and he can't contain himself! I email his teacher apologizing for sending my crazy son to school for her to deal with all day. I explain that his birthday is Friday and he can't handle the excitement. I also ask to bake cupcakes to send in for his birthday snack at school. Just add it to my list!

Kid party booked – check!
Invitations sent out – check!
Talked to teacher about cupcakes – check!
Talked to family about family party Saturday – check!
Bought *Wicked* tickets to take Max on Sunday to end his birthday weekend with a bang – check check!
Holy cow do we have a weekend coming up!

Max was thrilled with his kid party. Forget that all the adults were cold or that it wasn't the cleanest place. The kids had a ball climbing and Max had an awesome party! Forget my cleaning compulsions, I tucked them aside and watched all the kids have fun. Max barreled his way to the top and was beaming with pride. Seth got in on the climbing fun too. We put all the parents to work helping their kids climb. Sorry about that, parents!

I decide to let Max open his presents at the party. What on earth was I thinking? The kids all surrounded him, and I could barely see what he got through the craziness! Somehow, I managed to write down what he got. My advice is to open presents at home and to bring in one present at a time for your child to open so that you can stay sane and enjoy seeing each present.

We made it home to collapse. Ella woke up the next day with a fever, but what is new? My kids have decided to be sick all winter!

The family members all decide to come over despite Ella's fever and Max gets to have another birthday party with his family. He is loving all the attention, but Ella is not so happy and is asking when we will start planning her party!

Kid party a success – check!
Family party a success – check!

We drop Ella and Lillie off at my parents' house and venture off with Max to see *Wicked* at Shea's. Ella isn't feeling well and spends the day sleeping on my parent's couch.

We get to *Wicked* and it is packed! It is dark and loud, and I am reassuring myself that not only is Ella sick, but she would hate that it is dark and loud (I have to take a minute to tame some of my mommy guilt for not bringing her).

The first half of the musical is awesome, but Max is done. "What do you mean there is more?" My seven-year-old is annoyed that he has to stay. This is not looking good!

For the second half of the play Max hung on me, whined, complained and tossed and turned in his seat. I guess Seth and I should have gone by ourselves. The musical was awesome, but I can't wait to get out of there so Max stops complaining! He is now not feeling well and wakes up Monday morning with a fever as does Seth. Three family members down and two still standing!

Happy Birthday Max!
Happy Winter everyone!
Is it spring yet?

EIGHT CRAZY NIGHTS

I knew what I was in for...eight crazy, fun, memorable, exhausting nights! I had the house all decorated for Chanukah. We moved into a bigger house so of course this meant I had to go buy more decorations. My husband was already starting to twitch at the receipts piling up. He quickly drew up a spreadsheet and asked me to at least humor him and read it over. Seth wrote down every family member and teacher with an amount next to their name. Yes, I did glance at it.

I started shopping earlier than I normally do, thinking I would beat some of the crowds and be ready early! When I saw new *Frozen* merchandise, I started grabbing stuff and throwing it in the cart. I have two little girls who are *Frozen* obsessed, so I knew I'd better buy now! Unfortunately, my husband was with me giving me that evil eye. As any good wife would, I ignored him and headed to checkout.

I got the lecture at home about the girls being done, that I had already spent enough, and that it was time to move on to my son and the rest of our list. Seth has grown to realize how much fun I have in the little girl aisles. I know I am dangerous in a toy store. When I tell Seth, I am running to Target he tells me not to go crazy. Oh, how I love Target!!

I don't know how working mothers get all their shopping done. I was shopping for gifts every day on top of all the other work

I do every day. Every time I thought I was done we would remember more people to buy and bake for.

It has arrived, Chanukah was here, and all my children's gifts were wrapped and put in piles. My kids were off the wall excited and headed to school for their teachers to have to deal with their excitement all day. Those poor teachers!

Kids were home, latkes were cooking, candles were ready, dreidels were everywhere....let's do this!

The first night went smoothly and all the kids got their biggest gift, so they were very happy. Delicious latkes and donuts, blessings and the menorah, presents and a dreidel game. Chanukah was brewing!

The next day my son came home asking me for a Jewish Elf. What the heck was he talking about, a Jewish Elf? He was feeling some major jealousy about the fun antics his friends were telling him about the elf on a shelf. "Why can't you buy me a Jewish Elf Mommy?" Dagger in my heart! The look on his face! "I won't buy the Elf on a Shelf but there is a new Mensch on a Bench I will get you." His response: "That is creepy." Darn it!

Of course, the next day I am at Target buying more Christmas gifts we forgot. "How many people do we have to buy for? I mean aren't we blessed to have so many wonderful people in our life?" I see the Mensch on the Bench and decide I better text my husband before I spend 30 more dollars on something we really don't need. Mr. Unpredictable tells me to buy it.

I show Max the Mensch, we decide his name is Latke Larry, and the antics begin. My two-year-old is quickly trained to wake up and exclaim "what did Mensch do?" and run and find him. My favorite was when they found Mensch in a sink of marshmallows and began eating the marshmallows. Gross!

That night Max opens his Minecraft Mega Lego present. Ella opens her microphone and Lillie opens her boom box. It doesn't matter that Ella and Lillie have microphones; Lillie only wants what Ella has. The joys of having a little sister! Max has decided he is not thrilled with the $120 Lego present! I start lecturing him on the fact that Chanukah is about family and being together and I actually see my kids taking that in. Or I was happily delusional!

By the time I do Chanukah every night, and attempt to clean the house, I am going to bed later and later and getting crankier and crankier.

I look at my kids' piles that I wrapped and counted so well, and I start to panic that the rest of the little things aren't good enough. I can't bear to see them disappointed, so at 9 p.m. this exhausted mama ran to Toys R Us. Again, I found myself staring at toys texting Seth. He is less than thrilled that I am out spending more money. I get the lecture on buying small things. My blurry eyes grab some things and I head to stand in line.

Standing in line I start scolding myself for buying more presents and spoiling my children. I start picturing their smiles and shove my discomfort away. I run home to wrap more presents and gear up for two more nights of Chanukah. At midnight I literally fall into my bed.

We have two more fun nights. We spent every night together and with family. We had dinners, desserts, played lots of dreidel games, said lots of blessings, danced, sang, read Chanukah stories, and so much more! I saw how happy my kids were and I shoved away that exhausted feeling.

On the last night I asked my kiddos what their favorite part of Chanukah was. I didn't get the list of things...Max and Ella both told me they loved time with family! My two-year-old screamed "Mensch." I smiled. It was eight crazy nights and we made some good family memories. Now to get some sleep!

Happy Holidays!

MORNING MADNESS

Monday morning!

My two-year-old had woken me at 3 a.m. to come into my bed and woke me up five more times since then with hard kicks to my stomach, shoulders and face. She beats me up! I wake in a panic at 7:40 because my husband's alarm didn't go off. Of course the two-year-old is cuddled close to me looking oh so peaceful after hours of thrashing.

I throw on whatever clothes I can find as quickly as possible and run down the stairs to find my seven and five-year-old playing. I bark at Max to get dressed and throw clothes at him. He complains that he is not ready to get dressed, and I tell him to do it anyway. Why, oh why do we have the same conversations every morning? I need a morning chart. I taught this. I know!

I ask my kiddos what they want for breakfast and they tell me they aren't hungry yet. Is this Groundhog Day? I tell them they have five minutes to make a decision on what they want to eat, and I run to begin packing lunches.

I grab the peanut butter and jelly and throw it on the counter as my five year old yells that she wants to sit with her friend so I can't pack her peanut butter. Okay, Plan B. Seriously, I can't keep up with them!

I begin my son's sandwich, as he yells to me that he doesn't want a sandwich, he wants rolled up meat. (They have radar) Okay, forget the bread!

They stroll into the kitchen with their breakfast requests. I put lunch on hold and heat up pancakes that I made the night before for Ella and begin making Max a protein shake. I brush Max's hair while he is drinking his shake, as he hears his friend at the door. Max's friend's parents have to get to work so he comes over sometimes before school. I warn Max that Lillie is sleeping and he can't be his loud crazy self.

Max is in the playroom drinking his shake and playing with his friend. Ella is at the table eating pancakes, and my husband comes down dressed for work. Max spills his shake in the playroom and screams for me. I go running, thinking how my schedule does not allow for time to clean up his shake. By the way, where is Seth and why does he keep disappearing?

I go back to making lunches and yell to my husband to please get Ella dressed. "Please for the love of G-d help me," is what I want to scream, but I try my best every morning to be sweet. Sending my husband off to work and kids off to school on a good note is always my goal. It's not always achieved, but it's always the goal.

My husband says he needs lunch so I begin packing his lunch with as much food as I can find. I couldn't bear to hear Seth come home from work one more day complaining he didn't have enough food, so I took over making his lunches. Just add it to my ever-growing list of to-do's every day! My husband is one of those people who is thin and eats whatever he wants and as much as he wants. Yes, I can't stand it, it is so completely unfair! He is busy trying to eat enough during the day as I count my calories. Grrrrr!

Lunches are packed, snacks are packed, homework is packed, on to dealing with Ella's hair.

"Ella, time for hair and teeth," I yell. "I didn't have enough time to play," she yells back every morning. "Come anyway," is the daily response.
Groundhog Day!

Ella huffs and puffs stomping her feet into the bathroom. I ignore her attitude and start spraying her hair with something to protect her hair from lice. I got the dreaded note from school that there is lice in her class and I freaked out! Ella complains about the smell of the spray and I move on to pulling her hair up into a ponytail.

"I want to wear my hair down," she complains to me. "There is lice in your class so therefore you will never wear your hair down. Do you want bugs in your hair?" I ask her as she quickly quiets down. We have this same conversation every single morning. How does this child not remember why I am putting her hair up? Maybe just maybe, tomorrow she will remember!

Ella and Max brush their teeth. Max gets toothpaste all over the sink and counter, and all over his face and shirt. I take a deep breath to attempt to stay calm.

"Max, your future wife is not going to be happy with me if I don't teach you to be neater!" Yes, I did just say that and yes, we both giggled, which is much better than yelling at him, which is what I wanted to do.

I run upstairs and grab Max a new shirt. He throws on his new shirt while protesting that the toothpaste-stained shirt was fine. "I am not sending you to school with toothpaste on your shirt!" He disagrees but sees that I mean business.

We find all their shoes, hats and coats and begin the winter dressing process. Is it spring yet?

I help Max tie his shoes while reminding him to have us practice tying after school. I never remember, he never remembers, but I say it almost every day. I think today we will actually work on it. Add it to my list!

Ella brings me her pink sparkly cowgirl boots to help her put on. I calmly explain that she has gym and I need her to go find her *Frozen* sneakers. She stomps off to get her sneakers and I find myself once again taking a big deep breath. "Stay calm Mama," I tell myself. They will be out the door in T minus two minutes. I can do it!

They throw on their hats and coats and Max, his friend, and Ella climb into Seth's car. My fabulous husband gets major points for driving my kiddos to school almost every day. Yes, my five-year-old is petrified of the bus, and if you know me you know I have zero desire to make her try the school bus.

Have you seen what happens on a school bus? I will take a pass. Max also gets very bus sick like I used to.

I did it! Four out the door, two more to go! I run upstairs with 20 minutes to get Lillie and me ready and out the door. Makeup and jewelry are flying everywhere. I look presentable (I hope) and I run to my bed to wake the sleeping toddler with a diaper and clothes. I wake her up and wrestle her to get her dressed. I tell Lillie she has school and she cheers up and runs downstairs with me. I throw her hair in a pony, throw on our boots and coats, and throw her in the car.

I remember that we haven't eaten, and I throw an organic pop tart and almond milk at Lillie in her car seat (I am the crazy organic mom who spends too much at the grocery store). I grab a protein bar for me, and we are on our way. I forgot my coffee, I want to cry, but I continue to school anyway. I can start my day without coffee. I can do it!

I run into nursery school a little late and bring Lillie to the playroom. She giggles and runs around, and like I do every Monday, I tell my friend how I feel like I just put in a full day! We laugh and exchange morning stories. I look at Lillie laughing and smile while remembering that my crazy morning will start all over tomorrow.

I text my mom after nursery school with a picture of Lillie telling her Lillie loved school, but the mornings before school suck. She tells me that before I blink my house will be too quiet, so I should enjoy it. Just like I will have to remind Ella why she is wearing her hair up tomorrow my mother will have to remind me tomorrow to embrace my crazy!

P.S. My husband discovered that the two-year-old had turned the sound off on our alarm so hopefully tomorrow it will actually go off.

A DAY WITH MY TWO-YEAR-OLD

I get the big kiddos off to school and hear Lillie crying upstairs. So much for any alone time! I bring Lillie down and feed her and get her all set up with a cartoon as she slowly wakes up.

I am dying to get myself in the basement to jog on the treadmill, but the two-year-old is screaming she doesn't want to go in the basement. I know, I know, "Who is in charge?" My husband asks me this on a daily basis. Clearly Lillie is!

I decide to put on my boot camp DVD and get in a much-needed workout. Lillie is quickly on the floor with me doing push-ups, sit-ups and jumping jacks. She loves to work out with me, which is definitely adorable unless she is slapping me in the face as I try to do a sit-up!

I drag Lillie upstairs because I can't bear to wait till Seth gets home to take a shower. Lillie is happily dancing to *Bo on the Go* on the iPad and I take the fastest shower I can and get us both dressed.

We are heading out the door! We made it to the car! I ask Lillie to help me shop at Party City and she is all excited for two minutes. Then she starts screaming for Rolly Pollies. She doesn't care that she doesn't have class today – it is all I hear for the next two hours!

Lillie happily helps me pick out stuff for Max's birthday party at Party City and the Dollar Store. Other than throwing her hat, mittens and scarf on the floor repeatedly, it was pretty successful!

I never take Lillie out for lunch just the two of us, so I decide to go to Panera with her. She loves it there and so do I. I am starving, this will be quick, and then we can grab the stuff I need next door at Wegmans.

Panera is completely mobbed. There is nowhere to sit so I get our order to go. Lillie is screaming that she wants to stay. A table clears and I get us all set up. Now Lillie refuses to eat and is screaming she wants to paint. I ask her to eat and then we will go home to paint. She pushes her food away and I eat my salad as fast as I can because I need food. For the love of G-d Lillie let me eat for two minutes!

Lillie continues to scream to paint. I attempt to calm her and tell her she can paint soon and now she is crying.
Why did I think this would be a sweet lunch with my baby?

I hurry and pack us up because Lillie is going to disturb the whole place. Coats, gloves, hat, scarf, and Lillie is now screaming that she wants to stay and eat her food! Is she kidding me?

I rush her to the car and into her car seat. She is screaming to paint, and I know attempting Wegmans is not in the cards. I am sweating, exhausted, and can't believe it isn't even 1:00! I drive home taking deep breaths and see that Lillie is now fast asleep. So, I will sit here in the car with her and soak up the silence.

I will write and read and take deep breaths and enjoy an hour of no one yelling at me.

HAPPY FAMILY GAME NIGHT

I bought my eight-year-old *Apples to Apples Junior* for his birthday. This is my kids' latest obsession. They want to play every night, which is adorable.

I walk away from the huge pile of dishes to play with them. My husband is already cranky so I am already guessing this is not going to go how I would like it to!

I start passing out cards to everyone. The two-year-old takes her cards and quickly decides she wants to play while sitting on the table. It doesn't even faze me, but Seth wants her on her chair, so Lillie is now crying and running over to me. Happy Family Game Night!

Ella insists on being the first judge and picks Max as the winner. Seth is the next judge and also picks Max as the winner. Max is very persuasive, so this is the perfect game for him. Ella is now in tears because Seth picked Max. I am now holding Lillie on one leg crying and Ella on my other leg crying. I put Lillie in her chair and attempt to talk to Ella.

I am a social worker, so on a regular basis I attempt to teach my children important life lessons. I explain to Ella that she can't cry every time we don't pick her. I like that she wants to win, but she needs to have good sportsmanship and be happy for other people too. She calms down and we continue to play.

Max is rocking back and forth in our nice dining room chair. Seth asks Max to sit still or he will end up breaking another chair. (Max is very rough on our furniture!) Lillie climbs up on the table and I put her back in her chair. She throws herself to the floor and has a temper tantrum. We attempt to keep playing. Happy Family Game Night!!

We do another round and Max picks Ella as the winner. It is now my turn to judge, and I see Seth turning red watching Max rock on his chair. I ask Max to please stop rocking and he explains he has too much energy. We tell Max he will jog on the treadmill after this game because he needs to expend some energy. Max continues to rock, and Seth tells him he lost his iPad the rest of the day! Max stomps off saying he will go play with Lillie.

Seth wins the first game, and Ella is crying saying she wants another chance. Despite my better judgment I say, "One more round." Seth is rolling his eyes and quickly says he is out of this game. He goes off to entertain Lillie, and Max comes back.

Ella, who is just learning to read, keeps shoving cards in my face and sitting on top of me. She is now shoving a card in my face and bending it. I gently shove Ella off me, and she starts crying hysterically. I know her feelings are hurt, and she is the sweetest thing, so I feel terrible. I hold Ella and apologize and explain that I am feeling smothered and I don't want them bending and breaking cards to a brand-new game (that Lillie already spilled water on).

I calm Ella down and we decide to move on to snack time and book time because clearly, we are all melting down. Hopefully we will have better luck tomorrow!

MAX'S 8TH BIRTHDAY

I tell Max we will buy him an awesome present instead of a party. Max says, "No way." He wants a big fun party. Lucky me!

I begin to make the guest list, but you all know how crazy this is. School friends, soccer friends, family friends, neighborhood friends....my lists are always out of control and my husband usually gets annoyed with me (because he pays for it).

Max is begging for LASERTRON, but when we look up the price Seth quickly vetoes it and a few other places. The three of us fight about places and then Max thankfully chooses the YMCA. Soccer, dodgeball, food and fun. I can do this!

Max says he only wants boys at his party. Yes, he has girl friends. Yes, we probably upset people. Yes, only boys makes my list much more manageable!

The list is done, the place is booked, and I feel like I have already been through the ringer.

Max is obsessed with Minecraft and wants it as his theme. My friend Ashley was going to make Max an amazing Minecraft cake. I am a Pinterest mom (don't shoot me), and I scroll through Pinterest wanting to do ALL the Minecraft party ideas. My husband tells me I am nuts but then says he wishes I had planned his childhood parties. Max comes home from school and sees all the Minecraft ideas on the computer every day and is getting more and more excited!

I am sending things to Seth at work daily for him to print (our printer is not hooked up) and Seth is increasingly annoyed as I tell him he needs to print more and bigger labels.

All Max can talk about is his birthday. He is so excited and is bouncing off the walls. I am guessing his ability to sit still at school may be compromised this week as Max counts down to his party. Happens every January!

Ella, my five-year-old is so tired of hearing about Max's birthday and is growing increasingly jealous. If I hear about one more idea about Ella's birthday I am going to explode. "Ella, let me get through Max's party and then I promise we will plan yours!"

Party day arrives and I can't wait to get it done. I am hoping all 25 boys have a blast. It is Friday night, and at the end of the week I usually want to curl up on the couch and decompress, but I am gearing myself up for 25 crazy energetic boys!

The boys start piling in and my eyes bulge out of my head seeing all these kids. My husband, my parents, Seth's dad and his girlfriend, and a few of my friends stayed to help (thank G-d)! They don't stop coming in! We think we have most of them, so we head in for soccer in the gym. The boys just keep coming! What did I do? The last boy finally piles in and they happily (mostly) play soccer and dodgeball. Thankfully only one boy was injured. He sat on the side with a twisted ankle but quickly recovered (phew)!

We head into the party room and pizzapaluza begins! All the adults are handing out pizza, chicken fingers, subs, pop and juice. I realized how much  three years of waitressing prepped me for situations like these.

We move onto cake and I convince myself to cut the beautiful Minecraft cake because what other option is there? I am running around serving cake. I am over-stimulated, overwhelmed and I have frosting all over me. A friend looks at me and asks if I am going to do presents. For the love of G-d, yes, we are, and I am getting to it. (Sorry friend, and yes, I did snap at her!)

Presentpaluza begins and the boys are all screaming every time Max opens a present. Max got awesome presents! Our friends are so generous!

Another party is completed! Moving on to planning Ella's.

P.S. I am reading this 5 years later and laughing at the PINTEREST mom who planned Max's 8th birthday. Max is now 13 as I edit this, and PINTEREST mom is now TIRED mom!

TRIP TO VIRGINIA

Heading to Virginia, my home away from home. Seth and I both have one brother and they happen to live in Virginia. We love going to Virginia and getting to see our brothers and their families.

My brother was putting on an amazing seminar and my husband Seth was going to speak at it too! I wasn't even going to have to stay home with the kids. I was going to the seminar and I was so thrilled!

Packing for five people beyond sucks, but I got it all finished and we were ready to roll! We won't mention the list of stuff that we forgot, which is so not like me. When you pick up your daughters from bed and put them in the car you probably shouldn't forget their coats when it is below zero outside. Oops!

7:15 a.m. and we are on the road to Virginia. It was an extremely smooth ride. We didn't make one wrong turn and the kids watched movies and listened to music. An easy breezy long drive (unlike the ride home)! Seth also decided to drive the whole way so he didn't have to deal with the kids' demands and I could navigate.

The trip was amazing, wonderful and magical! My wonderful mom and my brother's sweet nanny stayed home with the five kids while the rest of us ventured off to the best seminar I have ever attended. My brother Corey and my husband Seth are on fire on stage! The two of them will continue to inspire, teach, help and change people professionally and personally! My heart is swelling with pride and I can't stop smiling. I am so happy to be there, and eleven hours later I realize that it is okay to take eleven hours for myself and my brother and my husband. It does not always have to be about the kids! I hope you all reading this know this. You can do things for yourself! I need to keep telling this to myself and all of you!

The next day my legs are toast from standing and jumping at the seminar in heels. My brother asks me what the outcome is. Are you kidding me? You inspired over 100 people! You changed lives, and you are asking me what your outcome is? I am shocked he's asking me this question.

The next day I watch the cousins play and I savor every moment. Ella is already telling me she doesn't want to leave. I know, I agree, part of my heart lives in Virginia!

I think the reason the rides home suck so much is because I don't want to leave. I am grumpy and my sweet husband has to deal with me. I am bitching because the DVD players and the backup DVD players aren't working. How am I going to make it eight hours home with no movies for the kids? I go on and on for four hours about how I wanted the car with a built-in DVD player. Sorry Seth, I know this was not pleasant!

I continue to try to get the DVD players to work for many hours to come. Seth figures out a wire is broken and is now looking up Targets within our vicinity to go buy new ones. The man is desperate to shut Lillie and me up with a movie!

I get confused and we end up on the 70 headed home instead of the 15. The GPS is taking me on a different route, and I decide to go with it. I am so mad at myself that I missed the 15 turn-off and I bitch and complain about it endlessly because I am WAY too hard on myself. Note to self – your children are watching, and you are teaching this to them. Maybe, just maybe, I could learn to go with the flow better!

We are at Wendy's and I see Seth is brutally tired from driving, and Lillie and my bitching. Max is actually winning the best behavior award and Ella is not far behind. Lillie is bored and begging me for *Frozen*.

I take over driving, and Seth gets our old DVD player to work! It is a miracle and I couldn't be happier. Peace the rest of the way home!

I drive the rest of the way while the kids watch movies. Seth says he is buying new DVD players for our next car trip in March.

We make it home safe and half sane! It was another whirlwind of a weekend. I am already missing my brother and his family, and the kids are asking when we will go back. When we buy new DVD players! Happy Traveling!

The seminar taught me so many things. My lessons:
Your passion is your purpose – go after it!
Show up with your best self!
We can do anything we set out to do!

My drive home lessons:
Let things go!
Go with the flow!
Be easier on myself!
Visit my family more often!

ELLA'S BIRTHDAY BONANZA

My children talk about their birthday ALL year long! Ella in particular cannot wait for her birthday. She cannot stand when it is anyone else's birthday. Birthdays have gotten way out of hand. First there is her actual birthday, then there is a family party, and then you can't forget about a kid party!

Ella complained the whole time I planned Max's January birthday. She complained it isn't fair that Max's birthday is before her birthday. She complained that she has to wait until March. She complained that she wants to be the oldest. So fun!

It is the night before Ella's birthday, and I am decorating the dining room, blowing up balloons, and putting out clues for her scavenger hunt. This is all becoming a tradition. My kids wake up to balloons in their room and then have clues to follow to find their presents. I buy presents for all three kids. (Yes, that's nuts, and Seth does not agree with this.)

Ella loves pancakes so I got up early to make her homemade fresh birthday chocolate chip pancakes. She eats her pancakes, puts on a beautiful sparkly dress, and heads off to school.

My mom takes my two-year-old Lillie, and I head to school to surprise Ella to have lunch with her and read a book to her class. I am exhausted, I want to hide and sleep, but I push myself to go to school.

The birthday fun day continues, and Ella is now asking me endlessly when her family and kid parties are. This is going to be a long week!

Ella decides she wants her family party at the Crab Shack so she can dance with the waitresses. How do I argue with that adorable request? "Ella, you don't like seafood. Are you sure about this?" Ella has mac and cheese at the Crab Shack for dinner, but man did she boogie with the waitresses! The service was slow, the food was just okay, but Ella was smiling. This is always my goal. Our parents are trying to be good sports about it. Max was thrilled to eat an entire steam pot and part of mine.

Note to self: family celebrations at home!

Ella is now relentlessly getting impatient for her kid party. I can do it. I can get through this week! Have you noticed I give myself a lot of pep talks?

I wanted Ella to invite a few friends over for a spa party. My friend said her assistants would do it for me. I couldn't convince Ella. She was determined to have a YMCA party like her brother. Seth was lecturing me that this is about Ella, not me. Yes, excellent point, BUT I DO ALL THE WORK! Ella would love a spa party. Next year!

I reluctantly booked the YMCA. She doesn't want a pool party, she doesn't want the adventure room, she wants to run around the gym and play games. Sounds terrible, but okay Ella!

I was determined to have Elsa come surprise Ella at her party. The fabulous Elsa I saw at the Melting Pot restaurant was moving away, which ruins that plan! I was not going to hire just any Elsa. I got a really bad Cinderella for a birthday party – make sure you see a picture of the character before they show up! I learned that lesson the hard way.

Seth and I brainstorm and decide to see if someone from his office would be Elsa. Fortunately, Kristin said yes! We had our Elsa, now for a costume. I email a couple people who I think have a costume, but panic and feel time pressure, and order a costume from Amazon.

It is the morning of Ella's party. Seth drops the kids off at Hebrew school and comes back with two dozen roses. Seth knows it has been a crazy week. He knows we are about to go to a Purim carnival and then to Ella's party. He is being super sweet, and I know his roses are a pep talk for the day/week and I couldn't feel more appreciated and loved!

It is now an hour before the party and texts start rolling in from "Elsa" that the dress I ordered is used and stained! Seriously? I ordered a new dress! Good job Amazon! I try telling myself, "Don't panic, it will be fine. Ella won't notice a used stained dress!" Seth repeatedly tells me everything will be fine!

Party time! I go upstairs to show my friend where to put the amazing *Frozen* cake she baked for Ella. I come back down to the party to three kids crying. Apparently tag leads to injuries, so we switch to a different game. Ella is giggling and smiling, and I make myself focus on that. I am holding my breath as

Elsa tells me she is arriving in four minutes. I feel like a kid, I am so excited to surprise Ella!

"Elsa" walks in and she looks perfect! Gorgeous, amazing and Ella is thrilled! Ella is clueless to the stains. (Yes, I saw a couple, but the dress is still beautiful.) All the girls go crazy for Elsa and keep grabbing her hand. Kristin was such a good sport. She put tattoos on kids, took pictures with every kid, and helped Ella open presents. A success! Phew! Thank you, Kristin!

Ella races through opening up her presents despite my many efforts to slow her down. *Frozen* merchandise is flying...

Slippers
Ever after High doll
Princess palace pets.....
Ella is in her glory!
Lillie is screaming trying to open presents and Ella is not having it! The joy of sisters!

The food and cakes are almost gone, the presents are all opened, and Elsa has left the building! Seth, our parents and our friends cleaned everything up as I said goodbye to everyone.

The car is packed, another party in the books! We are home, I am full of adrenalin and finally eating and Seth is passed out on the couch! Parenthood! Amazing, fabulous and NOT EASY!

Huge special thank you's:
To my parents, Seth's dad and fiance, Seth and my friends for ALL of your help!

My dear friend for baking another amazing cake!
My dear friend who came to enjoy and take pictures!
Seth's VP of design Kristin for being a kick ass Elsa!
Seth for letting me do this and paying for it!
We are so blessed!

My greatest lesson: stop and smell the roses!

PRODUCTIVELY PAINFUL

Seth picks the kids up from Hebrew school and we decide to head to the mall. I want to get Lillie a mattress at Sears and I need a new dress.

We start at Sears and the kids are running around lying on all the mattresses. I am asking the salespeople about toxins in mattresses and they look at me like I am nuts. I am asking my two-year-old which mattress she likes. I think I am funny asking Lillie, but Seth is not amused. When you take Seth to a store he is on a mission. It is a mission to a quick decision and that is that! "How fast can we get this done?" That is the question Seth asks himself when we walk into a store.

I find a soft double mattress I like, and I am quick about it but Seth's eyes start bulging in sticker shock. He tends to underestimate what I spend on things. Seth told me today that a wife is the most expensive purchase you make. Smart man!

We decide to leave, and I guide them all to the Macy's dress section. I get them involved in helping me pick a dress and Seth is asking me why I didn't come by myself. Scrooge!

The kids go into the dressing room with me. Max asks why I am going in the handicapped dressing room. I tell him having children makes me handicapped and one of the women trying on clothes in her dressing room giggles at my humor. I guess I am not the only one who finds myself funny!

I rush through the dresses as quickly as I can. Ella announces me every time I put on a new dress. "Here comes Rebecca Greene wearing her first dress," Ella announces loudly to Seth as I walk out of the dressing room. This continues after each dress I try on! Lillie is very busy collecting random things from the floor – tags, hangers, stickers....

We decide on a black dress, pay and move on to JC Penney. Lillie is tired of walking and I forgot a stroller, so I carry Lillie through the store. Max whines that it is his turn to go to GameStop. He buys a couple Skylanders with his own money, and we rest with some Annie's pretzels. I stare at the spot where the food court used to be and tear up. No more food court. No more merry go round. No more play place for my kids. I had so many happy memories there. Really, they are putting in a Dick's there? I am so not pleased with this decision!

We head to the car and the kids moan and groan that we are headed to City Mattress. Lillie doesn't like her crib, and she needs a bed. Seth tells the kids he needs some sleep  and is buying a mattress today!

The man in City Mattress starts telling us about mattresses and I see Seth's head about to explode. I ask to see mattresses as politely as I can to move things along. The kids are lying on all the beds wanting to help. If only I could get Seth to humor them and include them. The man on a mission wants to be done and go home. You can imagine that I pick a mattress as quickly as I can and take them all home. I am on a mission to make my mission man happy and be done!

Next, I have to take Max to a birthday party. Seth looks at me and says "You aren't staying, right? Don't leave me!" I laughed hard and promised Seth I was just dropping Max off. I know Seth is completely toast by now! I know there is no way he is in a state to deal with Lillie. However, I got a dress and Lillie got a mattress. It was a productively painful day!

My lessons:
Include my children when I shop and make it fun for them!
Get Seth more down time and less shopping time!

In honor of Seth, my birthday man, Whinypaluza would like to wish him a super happy birthday! You are an amazing husband and father!

I love this man that I found playing in a princess castle with our two-year-old today!

I love this man who answers Max's endless relentless questions!

I love this man that marries Ella over and over and humors her!

You are one in a million Seth!

I love you so much! Happy Happy Birthday sweetheart!

GERMS BE GONE!

We had just done the mall and bought me a dress and Lillie a mattress. We were exhausted and counting down to a good night of needed rest.

I tend to pass out the minute my head hits the pillow. It drives my husband nuts because sometimes he struggles to go to sleep. I think I run so much all day that I run myself ragged, so sleep doesn't tend to be an issue for me.

I am asleep quickly and am awakened by Seth yelling "Ella!" Did I hear that correctly? I am so out of it because I was fast asleep. I hear Seth downstairs and I wonder if he has Ella there. I wander to her room and find her lying in puke. I am trying to figure out why Seth is downstairs, but he comes in her room with paper towels and soapy water. We get her up and cleaned up. We strip the bed and put new blankets on. I put her in bed, and she is fast asleep. I get to my bed and hear her throwing up again, so I go running. At least it is in the pot this time. I clean her all up and she falls back to sleep. I get in my bed and start to think. First, where did she get it? Second, how many more times is she going to throw up? I start mentally preparing myself for a rough night. So much for sleep! I am actually wondering if it is even worth it to lie down at this point. I also have heard since this night that kids were throwing up left and right at school and the nurse's office was full. So, there is no secret now where Ella got this!

Ella continues to cry the rest of the night. I climb in bed with her and rub her the rest of the night trying to calm her down. She is taking down water, she isn't throwing up, but she won't stop crying. Give me strength! I am so tired that I am in and out of consciousness. I see flickers of glowing light over Ella. I say thank you to whoever is working on her. Yes, I believe in angels, and yes, I think an angel was working on my Ella. Whatever psychic ability I inherited from my mom's side comes out in my sleep. I must have slept a tiny bit because I had dreams of Lillie throwing up. I said a prayer for the rest of us to stay healthy.

I climb out of Ella's bed in the morning and bump into Max. He is holding his head and asking me why the cats were crying all night. "Mom, I couldn't sleep, I kept hearing crying!" I explain that was Ella, and Max collapses on the couch. I call school to let them know the kids won't be there and start thinking about my day. Taking a sick day is a lot of work! I am supposed to bring snack to Lillie's class. I am supposed to work lunch at school. I was happy to get to work lunch with two of my friends today. So much for that! I am also angry with myself for thinking about what a good winter we had with such little illness. Did I jinx us?

I quickly go to my email and see my friend who was supposed to work lunch also has a sick daughter. I feel so badly but I email everyone that my daughter is also sick. Then another email rolls in that the third volunteer is sick with the stomach flu! What is going on? Germs be gone!

Ella, Seth and Lillie are fast asleep. I tell Max I will be right back and drag myself to the car in my pajamas. I drop the snack off to a friend to take to school and head home. I am laughing at what it takes to take a sick day!

I come home to Seth rolling out of bed. He is not amused that I brought snack to my friend and explains to me that school could have found something to feed Lillie's class. He also informs me that Lillie puked. Maybe I wasn't dreaming? Lillie wakes up totally fine. The girl is a feisty spitfire and it is serving her. I am also thrilled I have been giving Max, Lillie and Seth grape juice. Supposedly it keeps the stomach flu away. Ella refuses to drink juice. My delicate flower is a mess. Ella cries for the entire day. Give me strength!

I go on a laundry binge and do tons and tons of blankets and sheets. Germs be gone! I am loving the sanitizing option on my new washing machine.

Lillie's mattress arrives and Seth breaks down the crib. I am laughing to myself thinking not only do I have to deal with sick Ella tonight, but I also have to deal with Lillie's first night in a big bed! You just have to laugh and attempt to roll with things. Life is never dull!

Seth and Max are completely and totally exhausted and sleep through the night. I don't think either of them moved. Must be nice!

I hear Ella crying and go running. I sleep with Ella and then hear Lillie crying and go running to her. I play musical beds all night and in the morning I felt like I ran a marathon!

Seth and Max leave for work and school and around 10 a.m. my mom arrives with stuff for Ella. New thermometer, popsicles, etc. Mom/Grammy to the rescue! I am beyond thrilled to see her. 38 years old, and yes, I still love when she walks through the door. She assures me that she will go to work and come back soon. What is this thing called work that she has to do? You mean she can't stay here?

Ella's eyes are red, and I start looking it up on the internet. Do not look up symptoms on the internet! Worst thing you can do! I quickly get off the computer and reassure myself that Ella just has a fever. She is so weak, and I keep reassuring myself that she will be fine. Why do we let our minds go to crazy places? It is just the flu! Ella cries the rest of the day. I am forcing her to drink water all day. I am the water police!

My neighbor leaves Ella a care package. Gatorade and an assortment of crackers for Ella and Oreos for the healthy kiddos. A ray of sunshine! So sweet. She made me smile. I needed to smile! I love my neighbor.

I get into bed and completely lose it on Seth. I cannot go a third night of no sleep! I am tired and cranky and tell him he cannot sleep through the night. Yes, I know he needs to work. Yes, I know he needs to function and be productive at work. I don't care! I am feeling insane at this point and NEED some sleep!

We take turns and get through the night. Ella is crying less and wakes up with no fever! She asks me for food, and I can't stop smiling. Hope...one of my favorite words! She ended up being sick for six days. That was a long week!

Now to say a prayer that the rest of us stay healthy. Take your vitamins, eat well, wash your hands and get plenty of rest. Stay healthy everyone!

My parents' store:
Marlene and Phil's Vitamin and Herb Center gets me the greatest vitamins and herbs!

My greatest lessons:
Sleep! We all need lots of sleep. I think the time change really messed up Ella and brought her immune system down. Get your sleep!

It is okay to accept some help! Moms, friends, neighbors...take advantage of what's offered!

It will pass!

SHOE SHENANIGANS

Ella had been home from school for four days not feeling well. She didn't have a fever today but was weak. She told me she was bored and wanted to get out of the house. I couldn't believe it and I quickly put her in the car. Four days at home was making me stir crazy!

We are heading to a Bat Mitzvah soon, so I bought Ella and Lillie adorable matching dresses. I searched and searched for shoes in our house, but nothing fit them. These children are constantly growing! What nerve they have being in a bigger shoe size!

We head to Target. Ella and Lillie are thrilled to be out of the house, and they love Target!

We head to the shoe section as Lillie screams for the toy section. I get Lillie involved in picking out shoes. Silver *Hello Kitty* flats, clear *Cinderella* shoes, blue sparkly Elsa shoes and silver *Frozen* sandals. I start trying them all on Lillie. One pair of shoes and she is done and running away from me. I am now pinning down my two-year-old to see which shoes fit her. The sweat is pouring down my face and Lillie is screaming and crying. I am sure we were quite the sight!

Lillie loves the *Frozen* silver sandals and they actually fit! She is now running up and down the aisle giggling, she is so happy with her new shoes. She starts showing everyone who walks by her beautiful new shoes. She is refusing to put her sneakers back on, and quite frankly I don't think it is a battle worth choosing!

Ella refuses to get out of the cart at this point. I try the same *Frozen* silver sandals on Ella, and they fit. She is thrilled that they are *Frozen* sandals and smiles and goes to sleep in the cart.

Lillie and I walk through the store and she starts randomly grabbing Barbies and Lalaloopsy dolls. She then grabs a kid's shopping cart and starts pushing it through the store. We actually have several kid shopping carts at home. I need to start bringing one with us when we shop.

I grab new *Hello Kitty* toothbrushes (I always change toothbrushes when they get sick). Lillie throws some Easter candy in the cart. Ella is now whining to go home, and Lillie is screaming as I put back every toy she grabbed.

We get to the checkout and I see Lillie opening up a *Frozen* Easter egg filled with candy. The kid is obsessed with eggs! She watches *Surprise Eggs* on YouTube and watches people open up eggs and find toys inside. I grab and throw the egg away from Lillie. She is having a meltdown, but I don't even care. Sure, I feel bad for everyone around me, but I am so used to it that it doesn't faze me.

The sweet checkout lady engages Lillie in a conversation, Lillie calms down and we get through the line.

I am almost home free, but Lillie is now taking her sandals off, chucking them in the cart, and screaming for me to put her socks and sneakers on. With patience of steel I tell Lillie that she cannot talk to me like that and she apologizes. I put on her socks and sneakers and we head to the car. Thankfully the shoe shenanigans are over, and we can go home!

My Lessons:
Pick your battles!
Bring Lillie a shopping cart.
Buy new toothbrushes often.
Have patience of steel.

ANOTHER TRIP

If you remember our trip home from Virginia, we had some technical issues. Seth was prepared for this long car trip with new DVD players. Max and Ella better be ready to hear Lillie screaming for the movie *Frozen*!

I got all caught up on the laundry (don't faint). I was doing everything else except packing. I dread packing. I went back to making lists this time, but I do anything to avoid starting. Seth brings the suitcases up from the basement and I am forced to face the task at hand.

I spent a lot of time shopping in preparation for our cousin's Bat Mitzvah. New dresses, new shoes, new ties, new jewelry...coordinating family of five! Call me a cheeseball but I was so excited that we were all going to match. Our cousin called us "Shades of blue."

I was holding my breath for a smooth ride there and an easy weekend. Traveling with three children always feels like a big adventure. I kept thinking about the three-hour temple service we were going to Saturday morning, wondering how I was going to get through it with three young children. If I know I can't sit through a three-hour service, how are my kids going to do that?

It is the day before and I purge and spend the entire day getting ready for the trip. I spent hours and hours packing and realize the girls don't have cardigans (I thought they did), and we need snacks for the car. I also can't find my bathing suit or Ella's floatie for the hotel pool. Off to Target and Wegmans. I think most of the employees at Wegmans and Target know Lillie and I!

It is the morning of our trip and I am packing all the last-minute essentials. Seth is trying to set up the car DVD players and tells me it is missing a wire. Nothing like waiting until the last minute to check it out! I spend a couple weeks buying and preparing, and asked Seth to buy and take care of one thing. I was aggravated but Seth was assuring me he figured it out and it would be fine.

Seth decides to drive the whole way to Fishkill, NY because he knows if he is driving, he doesn't have to deal with the kids! He is a very smart man, that husband of mine. We get to a toll and Seth hands a credit card for the $14 toll. They don't take credit cards! Who leaves home without cash? Seth and I tend to have zero dollars on us. We search for money all over my car and come up with $7 and the guy lets us go. Phew! The kids took turns the entire trip asking me for snacks, drinks, movies, and complaining. It was long and painful!

You can imagine when we get there that the kids have tons of steam to let off, so we don't dare go out for dinner. We took the kids to the pool and let them burn off energy. I had no desire to swim but I knew I needed to buck up and do this for them.

Five people in one room is never easy. I catch myself and put myself in check that I am lucky and fortunate that we can afford to stay in a hotel and take this trip together. Maybe instead of being cranky and miserable I can choose to feel happy and fortunate. It is all a choice!

We get some sleep and I spend two hours getting us all nicely dressed and ready for Temple. We head to the service and I hold my breath wondering how the heck this is going to go. My son Max is called up to hold the Torah. He is on the Bimah for such a long time. He is behaving and being respectful and my heart is swelling with pride! Our cousin gets up to do all her parts and does an amazing job. I am smiling and happy to be here to witness this. She does her speech and it is sweet and meaningful and funny, and my two-year-old says our cousin is funny!

My girls did a great job in Temple! They read books, drew and danced, but they also listened to parts of the service and stayed as quiet as they could. I felt successful and I started to release my held breath.

We head to the nice luncheon and make it back to the hotel. We took a couple wrong turns, and I swore at Siri, but we made it. I was so worn out I actually fell asleep! I never nap. I hate napping. I needed a nap!

We get all dressed again and head to the Bat Mitzvah party. It was time to celebrate. Ella has her fun dancing with Daddy and then passes out before 8 p.m. Party pooper! My mother-in-law comes and sits with me, looks at Ella asleep on the chair and explains that the party pooper gene is genetic from her! I appreciated the laugh. Lillie fluttered around like a little social butterfly; giggling, dancing and talking to everyone. Then there is Max my little stud muffin. He danced up a storm.

The kid has some moves! He had 13-year-old girls dancing with him. I think we are in trouble with that kid!

Seth and I are loving our cousin's special day. We truly enjoyed the candle lighting, dancing and just being able to experience this with family. I was exhausted. I was also creating  memories I knew we would all remember!

The next morning, we eat breakfast at the hotel and then head to eat brunch with our family. If I give them two breakfasts maybe they wouldn't ask for food for a little while. Funny thinking, right?

We head for home and the swearing at Siri begins. Siri is telling me to take the 44 North, but there is only a west or east option. Siri drives me nuts. She is not quick enough for me. iPhone tends to do updates on Siri and make her worse in my opinion. I want to throw her through the window but instead I throw her at Seth and tell him to deal with Siri. Seth exits and says let's see how I do if I am nice to Siri. He magically gets us on the correct route. Siri likes Seth better!

Max is screaming his window won't open. We pull over and Seth and I cannot figure out how to open it. How many people will it take to figure out how to open a window? I will let you know.

We stop and get a snack and Seth takes over driving. The requests continue and the complaining doesn't seem to ever end. I turn to Seth and he reads my mind and says, "Next trip we are flying!"

Happy Family Time!

My lessons:
I need a break from long drives with my children!
Make sure I have everything I need for a trip ahead of time!
Print out directions (Siri annoys me)!
When possible, take longer trips that don't feel like a whirlwind!

AN EVENTFUL EASTER

We had a wonderful Passover Seder at my parents' house. My mom made a ton of delicious traditional food, and Seth led a funny yet meaningful Seder. The kids behaved, and we ate a ton and laughed a ton. All our parents were together, and we had a wonderful evening.

The next day Max starts complaining that he wants to go on an Easter egg hunt. I feel badly knowing how I felt as a kid.

Easter morning Seth is off to Wegmans with a list and I add Easter eggs and jellybeans to the list. Seth says no way and heads out. He returns with some odd jellybeans and no Easter eggs. I am not amused.

Max is whining that he wants to do an egg hunt. Seth looks around the playroom and starts collecting eggs. Our two-year-old is egg-obsessed, so I have been buying her random plastic eggs, but in Lillie fashion she has lost most of them.

I stomp up the stairs wishing I had gone to Wegmans. I don't enjoy when Seth goes, because he doesn't tend to come home with what I want. While I am upstairs Seth goes back to Wegmans (it is across the street). He calls me with egg and jellybean questions. I cannot believe we are discussing plastic eggs – which they are out of!

Seth comes home very annoyed with me. He tells me he is not doing any Christmas or Easter stuff. The kids and I decide we will buy more matzah and I can send them on a matzah scavenger hunt. I just like any reason to do fun stuff with my kiddos!

I look up the YMCA schedule online and it says they have open swim all day. I am surprised they are open, but I pack up and head there. I am going to work out, and then my family will meet me to swim. Why did I think a Christian-based organization would be open on Easter? Not a car in the parking lot. Time for plan B.

We head to the bowling alley. Max starts us out. He wants no guidance on how to bowl correctly and is running and throwing the bowling ball. All he wants is a spare and is throwing himself on the ground every time he doesn't like how he bowled. Seth and I are growing repeatedly annoyed with his behavior. I tell Max to just have fun. I ask Max if I can please teach him how to bowl. There is no talking or reasoning with Max!

Ella is the giggling bubbly bowler. She wants Daddy to help her and has a great time rolling the bowling ball between her legs. She is dancing around having a fabulous time and is getting a bunch of spares!

Max is hugging Ella when she bowls well which then turns to dirty looks as the game goes on. I tell Max that Daddy would be happy to help him too. I tell Max my dad still helps me bowl, but I can't seem to say anything right.

Max loves the vending machine, and is obsessed with looking at all his options, and asking me if he can have something.

"Max, if you behave and get it together bowling, and have some fun with us, I will let you buy something at the end of the game."

Bingo! I should have known. Max is my incentive man! Give Max an incentive to strive for and he will do whatever you want him to do.

It is my turn to bowl. Lillie wants to bowl so I let her roll my ball with me. Seth is not amused and wants to actually bowl a game with me and try to crush me. Oh, the joys of trying to make all my family happy! Note to self: don't try! Focus more on making myself happy!

Lillie is in a running-off stage. I remember this stage all too well with Max at this age. It is not fun. I vividly remember our Temple director finding me crying at Temple as I attempted to chase Max while pregnant with Ella. Good times!

Lillie is repeatedly running off and I am busy trying to protect her from all the flying bowling balls.

The game ends and Seth happily won. The kids are beyond thrilled to pick something from the vending machine.

Half the bowling alley is totally empty. The kids decide to run up and down over and over again. Seth and I take a seat and watch them run and burn energy. This continues over and over and Seth asks me why we spent money on bowling. All they want to do is run. If only I could bottle and sell their energy!

Happy Passover!
Happy Easter!
Happy spring!
Love, the Greene family

My lessons:
Call ahead on holidays to see what is open!
Go to Wegmans myself!
Give Max incentives to work towards when I want to improve
his behavior!
Leave Lillie with one of our mothers next time we decide to go
bowling!

A FRIDAY'S ADVENTURES

I jumped out of bed knowing the list of things happening today! I just went to my brother's amazing seminar, so I was pumping myself into a good state. I can do this!

I quickly get all three kids ready and run Max and Ella to the dentist for a cleaning. Smooth appointment – check it off the list, moving on!

I look across the street where one of my besties is a hairdresser, and we run over to give her a quick hug! I look down the street at Rolly Pollies and I shake my head realizing I am about to take my kids to school and bring my two-year-old right back here. Just call me the taxi service. I cannot seem to wrap my head around all the driving I will do today!

I ring the school's doorbell and realize I am clueless as to how to sign my kids in late because I have never had to. (Mental pat on the back for that one!)

Kids are off to class and I run home to grab Lillie and let my hubby run off to work. Two ships sailing in the night! "Hi honey," I kiss Seth as he runs out the door to work. "See you tomorrow," Seth laughs knowing we are simply playing pass the child today. I am so thankful that he runs his own businesses and does his best to help me when his schedule allows. Nothing compares to a somewhat flexible work schedule.

I feel like I have put in a full day already but Lillie's excitement to go to Rolly Pollies rubs off on me and I am smiling again. She has an awesome time and I feel like I got to spend some quality time with her. There is nothing like one-on-one time when you have three children!

I drop Lillie off with my mom and run off to school to organize and do Max's second grade Valentine's party (redo day because of all the cold and snow we keep getting). I am so over Valentine's Day!

Max walks in the classroom door from lunch and sees me there, and his eyes light up. This is why I do this! I have my four games to set up for the party and my son's teacher is asking me how to set up desks etc. 24 second graders excited for a party and I realize I have to actually attempt to think and organize. It is totally clear to me that all these screaming second graders aren't even fazing their teacher. The kids' excitement is contagious, and I can't wait to see them play all the games I planned!

Moms start pouring in (thank you moms). We all run the games and crafts, and the kids have sundaes and have an amazing party. My son is absolutely screwed after this teacher! He has set the bar so high, I fear for next year. "Enjoy the moment, enjoy the moment, stop thinking," I lecture myself.

Max and I go to grab Ella and we are off to nursery school to set up the book fair. Why do I volunteer for so much? I love my kids' schools! LOVE! That is why!

You may think I am a stay-at-home mom but in reality, I work for my kids' schools for free! This is where I want to be. Thank you, Seth! I know I could be making us a lot of money, but I will never get these moments back! My mom keeps telling me that work will always be there! My kids being little won't always be there!

I set up the book fair with other moms while my kids play with some of their friends. Dinner and a birthday party are left on the agenda. Two more things. I can do this! I am ready to fall over but I push onward. I've decided that moms have superhuman strength.

Seth picks up Lillie from my mom (without my asking him – major husband points- wow)!
Men – if you want your lady hot and bothered go do something helpful without her asking you first!
Women – if you want your man super happy tell him how awesome he is!

We meet at home and feed the kids dinner. I look at Seth and just laugh about this day. I kiss him goodbye and run Max to a birthday party. I want to go sit in Barnes and Noble alone with a book and a coffee, but I run back home so I can see my husband's face. Did I mention the three cups of coffee I have had today? I have a coffee addiction. I love coffee! I make a mental note to cut back and drink more water.

I come home and see my husband playing with Ella and Lillie. Mushy alert but I feel like I fall in love all over again at different moments. There is nothing like seeing Seth being cute with our daughters! I love watching him wrestle and be a great dad with Max but seeing him be sweet with Ella and Lillie is something else. Mushy moment over!

Time to get Max. I grab him and his friend and listen to them giggle the whole way home. Music to my tired ears! I pass his friend's house twice (it is dark, and I have only been there once). I get him safely home and Max is talking up a storm pumped full of energy at 9:45 at night. Uh oh!

Max, Seth and I decide to start watching *Maleficent* because the girls are asleep and won't be scared, and I am not going to attempt to put Max to bed knowing he is energized from the sugar and excitement.

I did it, I made it through, and I did a good job. Please give yourself some praise sometimes. You deserve it! Unfortunately, Ella got completely stiffed of my attention today. Mental note to give her extra attention tomorrow. (I find it irritating that despite all I did today, I still find a way to criticize myself. Do we ever give ourselves a break?)

Thanks for taking this Friday adventure with me. I am exhausted but I am happy!

My lessons:
It is okay to say no sometimes. I don't have to volunteer for everything!
I can't do this alone. Seth, my mom, and a bunch of other moms helped me through today!
Drink less coffee!
Stay present!
Carpool!

WE TOOK A "SICK DAY"

I pick Max and Ella up from school and Max has that look. He looks ill and clammy with no other symptoms. I think he has hit a wall and I know already he is going to try to get out of school tomorrow. I try to be tough (not in my nature) most of the time. I push myself to do what I think is the right thing as a good parent. I am a natural softy, if I am truly honest with myself.

It is the next morning and I walk into the family room and see Seth and Ella cuddled on the couch. The time change has absolutely sucked. Ella has been dragging all week and I see her lying there half asleep on the couch and the wheels start spinning that I should let her rest. I have been pushing my sweet girl all week to get up and get moving as she dragged herself around. My usual peppy princess was pooped!

Max comes climbing down the stairs and gives me that look! I know that look, it is the one that says, "Please don't make me go to school!" He doesn't have a fever, he isn't throwing up, but he looks ill. I have plans at 10 a.m. with my girlfriends that I was excited for. Sometimes being a mom really cramps my fun! I look at Seth and we call it – NO school today kids! Max is relieved and Ella looks completely confused. You know what, sometimes it is okay to rest. Sometimes it is okay to not push, push, push. My kids needed rest and it was obvious!

I started to tear up with frustration because sometimes I just want "me time." Sometimes I want "girly friend giggle time!" Seth being the amazing husband that he is rested with Ella while I pounded out my frustration on the treadmill and got to take a shower without any kids screaming at the door. Amazing how a shower by myself can completely make me happy. The little things I used to take for granted!

Seth heads out to work and I am left home with three kids. I cannot believe how easy it feels to have one child home with me every day while the other two are in school. It has spoiled me.

Ella and Lillie were already screaming and fighting about playing with all of Ella's new birthday toys. This was not going to be a fun day for me! Can you remind me why I let Max and Ella stay home today?

I let the kids have a lazy few hours and then arrange to go return stuff that I borrowed for Ella's party. I need to get out of the house. Max seems completely fine and I warn him that he is going to school tomorrow! After our drop-off we decide to go to Anderson's for lunch. Seth stops by to say hello and we run into one of my closest friends. The day was looking up. When things feel stressful at home, sometimes you just need to get out of the house!

Next, I arrange to meet my friend in a Tim Hortons parking lot to give her Girl Scout Cookies she ordered. Let me tell you about Girl Scout Cookies. Ella sold a ton. I am so proud of her! Now I have to find everyone to give them their cookies. I am going to get rid of all these cookies! My Type A personality is in full swing! I feel like I am dealing cookies in the parking lot.

My kids complain the whole time we wait for my friend. I threaten them that if they don't behave, we are going home, and they won't be allowed to go spend their Toys R Us birthday money. They quickly behave!

My friend gets her cookies and tells me I am nuts to go to Toys R Us with three kids. Yup, stamp nuts on my forehead most days. We are off to toy chaos!

I state my expectations that we stay together in the store and take turns looking at everyone's toy section.

We enter toy heaven and my kids are running! Max ends up with a sword and shield in his hands before I blink and then throws a rip stick in the cart. Lillie is just randomly throwing things in my cart and I am ignoring it. Ella is very upset and wants to make sure I know what Lillie is doing. Max asks me if I am buying all of it. I say "no" and keep walking. Lillie wants every Doc McStuffins thing she sees. Max is looking at Minecraft and Ella is complaining it is her turn.

I take them to Ella's section, and she throws a Lalaloopsy in the cart. How many dolls does this child need?

Lillie now has a small cart that she is filling with toys and Max is completely appalled by her behavior. I am now taking stuff out of my cart that Lillie keeps throwing in (sorry Toys R Us). I explain to Ella that she really doesn't need another Lalaloopsy. I turn to Max and tell him he doesn't need another sword. Ella has crates full of dolls. She agrees and heads to Shopkins. Max pleads his case that he wants swords for friends to have when they come over. (The kid is going to be successful because he is relentless, persistent, and I have to be in my firm Mama Bear stance to win against Max.)

Lillie follows Ella to the Shopkins and I feel my patience disappearing. It has been an hour in the store, and I need to leave. I have seriously hit a wall and I am trying my very hardest to stay calm. At this point I tell Ella and Lillie which Shopkins they are getting and walk to the register.

I hand the cashier gift cards and coupons and she looks completely overwhelmed. This isn't that hard! I want to ring myself out and my kids are acting completely crazy now. Lillie is opening candy, Ella is singing, and Max is running in circles! I grab Max and ask him to please stop running and focus on watching Lillie for me.

The cashier is really struggling with everything I handed her, and I start helping her. I hand her candy Lillie is opening to pay for it as I hold back my meltdown.

Max is going to be an amazing husband and father one day! He sees me holding back tears. He walks Lillie over to some toys and starts distracting her as I deal with the cashier. Somehow, I end up owing money. At this point if the cashier screwed up I don't even care! She apologizes to me and I pack my kids up and drag screaming Lillie to the car.

Lillie is having a full-fledged two-year-old tantrum in the car and Max tells her that if she gets in her car seat, I will give her the surprise egg I bought her (the one she started opening without permission). Max earned some major points, let me tell you! (Being an oldest child sets you up to be an awesome parent, if I do say so myself.)

The kids are buckled, I am headed home and I know not only will Seth be home soon, but I also have a meeting to go to tonight. A break is in sight and I can taste it!

I am glad I gave them the day off and yet I am completely and totally fried. Happy "sick" day!

My lessons:
Don't take three kids to Toys R Us!
When the kiddos are driving me crazy at home...get out of the house!
It is okay to let your kids stay home. We live in a world of push, push, push! It is okay to take a timeout from it.

SUPER-FILLED SUNDAY

The alarm goes off and I lecture myself to be a good Jew and get my kids up and ready for Hebrew school. Shouldn't Sundays be for sleeping in and relaxing??

Seth turns over and goes back to sleep with Lillie and I drag myself downstairs and get Max and Ella ready for Hebrew school as Max complains that it is a waste of time. I lecture him that we are honoring G-d going to Hebrew school. I did the same thing to my parents. This is payback.

I drop the kids at Hebrew school and head to the Y to get in a good workout. My friend texts me that they are heading to the zoo today. Seth says, "Let's do that," and he runs to get the kids while I run home to shower.

It is a beautiful Sunday and the zoo is packed. I just fed my kids a snack, but they complain most of the time at the zoo that they are hungry. Do my children ever stop eating?

We run to Max's first baseball practice. My fabulous husband decided to coach Max's team. He says I decided this, but it is so not true! Seth is a soccer guy. He loves soccer and loves to coach Max's soccer team. I love baseball. I talked Max and Seth into trying baseball again, and I laugh watching them smiling and enjoying themselves during practice. I have to stop asking my children, and just sign them up for things! For example, all my daughter Ella does is dance around the house, but she doesn't want to take dance lessons. I am signing her up for dance class. I'm not asking.

Max complained last year because he was on a team filled with kids from another school. They were nice kids and it was nice to make new friends. Max wants to play with kids from his own school, so I made that happen. I handed Seth a list of kids from Max's school for the baseball meeting and off he went to work his magic. I don't think I will hear Max complaining this year. We shall see!

My girls play on the playground, Seth runs practice, and we finally head for home. My kids run outside to play with the neighbors and Ella decides it is time to go door-to-door to collect food for the food pantry (per Girl Scouts request). I have been running all day but what is some more running? It is for a good cause, right!

I head inside to cook breakfast for dinner (Ella's favorite) and then go nuts vacuuming crumbs due to all the ants I am finding. I love spring, minus the ants. It happens every year. Go away ants!

The kids are sunburned and melting down. We are all exhausted. Signing off on a super-filled Sunday!

Happy spring everyone!

My lessons:

Always carry lots of food for my vultures – I mean children!
Stop giving them so much power and sign them up for stuff I
think they will enjoy.
Slow down maybe a little.
It's time to restock our sunscreen.

WHEN DADDY IS AWAY

It is Monday and I know the week ahead is going to be challenging. Seth is traveling all week! I am going to have major mommy duty!

I get the kids ready. Seth takes Max and Ella to school, and I take Lillie to school. Seth is off to the office and then New Jersey for a meeting.

Lillie and I have a nice time at school together. Her two-year-old antics were kept to a minimum, and my Lillie Rose enjoyed flower day at nursery school.

I drag Lillie to the stitching place to drop off baseball shirts for Max's team. The guy is asking me letter questions, pants and sock questions and I am clueless. I was just asked to drop off shirts.

I run to my parents to put their ladder back in their garage. I borrowed it to get Max's toy axe down from the roof. I don't make this stuff up. Don't even ask! Max somehow threw it on the roof and has been obsessing over getting it down. Seth would not let me climb on the roof. He is no fun! I borrowed said ladder for nothing! By the way, we need to buy our own ladder!

We venture to my least favorite place – Walmart. I get everything on my list, including a football for Max's teacher. I am so thankful for self-checkout because I don't have to deal with the crazy long Walmart lines. Now off to Max and Ella's school.

I walk into school with Lillie, and Max's class is so excited to see her. I get everyone in Max's class to sign the football for their teacher for teacher appreciation week. I drag Lillie away from Max and his friends to go hang artwork for Arts Fest. I am the least artistic person. I probably should go nowhere near artwork. I do my best to hang things. My Type A personality doesn't tend to kick in with art. My kids don't enjoy art class. I can't imagine where they get that from (I was the same way). I appreciate a lot of things as an adult that I did not enjoy when I was younger – art, history, economics to name a few. I am ashamed to say I definitely did not pay attention in many classes. I remember my first psychology class and thinking "YES, finally a good class that I am interested in!"

Lillie starts to melt down (she has been so good) so I get her some Timbits and let her relax at home before we have to go grab Max and Ella. I have created a Timbit monster! I go through the drive-thru to get coffee and Lillie screams "Timbits." I drive past Tim Hortons and Lillie screams "Timbits." Uh oh, I think someone has a Timbit addiction and someone has a coffee addiction!

My kids go running to the playground after school and I am completely freezing. It is April 27 and I've put my winter coat and winter boots away. What was I thinking? I need my big huge warm coat on the playground today! I refuse to wear my winter coat in April, and man am I paying for it. My kids aren't fazed but I finally drag them away because my hands were going numb!

We head to Dash's with our friends. Seth is away and I don't have anything to cook for dinner. The kids order food and do their homework and we hang out with our friends. Ella is royally mad that I forgot her Barbie and Lillie is screaming and refusing to share her cash register with Ella.

Ella freaks out about Max's soccer practice. She does not want to go with us to practice and I don't blame her. Thankfully my parents let me drop off Ella and Lillie, and Max and I run to practice. You would think I would have pulled out my winter coat, winter hat and gloves. Don't I ever learn? Come on spring, where are you? Come back!

Max and I run to get Ella and Lillie and head home. Snack, PJs, TV, book time for my kids. I get them to bed and work on my broken sink (that I have now made worse). It has been quite a day! My husband is now flying home, but he is heading out again Wednesday. I am sure I will have more fun crazy chaos to share!

My lessons:
Keep up with my kids.
Travel with Ella's favorite Barbie.
Appreciate my hardworking husband.
Realize I am stronger than I think.
Keep lots of toys and snacks on me to keep Lillie happy.

What I want my kids to know:

Max — seeing you laughing with your friends in lunch today melted my heart. You're a social butterfly, quite the soccer player, and you whiz through your homework because you are so bright! I am so proud of you!

Ella — the principal stopped me in school today and asked if Lillie is as happy and peppy as you. You are so happy, and it glows from you! Your teacher told me everyone in the school knows who you are. My happy sweet girl, my Ella Rae of sunshine!

Lillie — I treasure my days with you! Mommy and Me school, art class, music, Rolly Pollies gym and lots of Wegmans and Target trips. I have a great time with you. I love to see you giggle! You wrap your arms around me and squeeze. You are so lucky you are so cute!

DADDY STILL AWAY! BOOHOO!

Ella went to bed with a fever, so I keep her home even though she doesn't seem to have a fever today. It is Thursday and I knew it was going to be a long week without Seth.

My friend texts me about taking Max to school. I love her for so many reasons, the list is endless. I have met some amazing women hanging out at the playground after school every day with my kiddos. My kids look forward to the playground every day and I look forward to seeing my friends!

Max is off to school and Ella and Lillie are playing. Ella is busy painting, and Lillie is screaming to play with her pink slime. I get them both situated with their stuff and head to do dishes. I leave the kitchen to go check on Ella painting and Lillie starts screaming. I run and find her attempting to take the slime out of her hair! What did she do? Slime is all over her hair. I rip it out as she screams louder. It is not coming out! I drag her upstairs crying and put her in the tub. I use shampoo to try to scrub it out. Fortunately, the shampoo is loosening it, and I can comb it all out. I get Lillie out of the tub, which is now full of slime. I scrub the tub, get Lillie dressed, and head back downstairs to do laundry. I am completely exhausted. Motherhood is absolutely exhausting. I didn't know what exhaustion was before I became a mother!

My clean, dressed child proceeds to eat a peanut butter and jelly sandwich and smear it all over her nice new clean clothes! How many outfits and messes will we go through today, Lillie?

She is now naked again and throwing toys all over the kitchen for me to trip on. When my husband sees me admiring an adorable baby, he tends to remind me that they become crazy toddlers. What happened to my sweet adorable baby? She has become a feisty, spirited two-year-old. She is lucky she is so cute!

Lillie is now dressed again, and Ella has moved on to doing her homework. There is hope that she is going to school tomorrow and I can go on Max's class walk. I would say this is a horrible week for Seth to be away but isn't every week?

I tell the girls I need to go to Wegmans and Ella has a fit. I need my mom to save me. I am in desperate need of a break. "Mom, take these kids away from me!"

I drop Ella and Lillie with my mom and head to Wegmans. My friend takes Max home with her. It absolutely takes a village. I could not be a parent alone! All my kids are taken care of and I enjoy the silence in the car as I head to errands.

I go get the girls and eat dinner with my parents. I go get Max and drag him away from his friend. Four hours wasn't enough. It is never enough!

Heading home and knowing that bedtime is almost here. Seth texts me that he and my brother went out for Japanese food.

No fair! Seth is at a conference hanging out with my brother going out for meals! He could be a little more sensitive.

When I married Seth, I told him I did not want a husband who traveled for work. So much for that deal! I see clients wanting to fly him out to meet with them. I see how Seth glows and grows from his work conferences. I have to buck up and be a supportive wife. Three more days...I can do it!
I need a Cosmo!

Lessons:
Monitor Lillie!
Expect and accept messes!
Be flexible – go with the flow of life!
Be thankful for all the great people in my life!
Support my husband's work ventures!

Max – if you want more play dates you should probably be easier when I pick you up!
Ella – eat your fruits and vegetables and be healthy!
Lillie – maybe you could keep things out of your hair!

MY DRAMA KING

It is May 1 and an absolutely beautiful day outside. I am up early and gearing up to get all the kids ready and get to school to go on Max's spring walk with him. Ella is bummed she can't come but Lillie is excited to walk with Max.

All the second graders in the school start heading to the bike path with all their teachers and tons of parents. Max is full of energy and curiosity and is investigating wherever we walk. He has the magnifying glass out and is looking at everything. Max is climbing and driving me absolutely nuts because he is not listening and staying with me.

Lillie is behaving and staying in the stroller and I am doing my best to keep up with Max. There are tons of kids everywhere.

I am walking on the path, Max is running off the path and I hear him scream: "It's in me, it's in me!" I run full speed ahead and my Mama Bear adrenalin rips the stick out of Max's foot without a thought. The stick went through his sneaker into his foot. I am very thankful Max's teacher put the first aid kit in my stroller! I rip off the sneaker and bloody sock, grab some gauze and stop the gushing blood. What am I going to do?

My friend comes up to me and takes Lillie and tells me to go ahead and bring Max to the nurse. I push all 72 pounds of Max all the way to the nurse's office, full speed ahead in Lillie's stroller. Max whined the whole time. I checked his foot. The blood had stopped. I told Max I didn't even think he needed stitches, and it could be so much worse! Mr. Drama continues to cry and whine and the nurse cleans him up. Max is telling me he needs to go home and lie down. The nurse says Max is okay, and we can go meet everyone. Max looks at me like the nurse has five heads.

I race back to find Lillie who seems confused when I find her. She keeps asking me what happened and why did I take her stroller? She continues to ask me the same questions 10 times. She happily gets back in her stroller and Max limps back to school,

I leave Max at school and say a prayer that he is okay and doesn't drive his teacher totally nuts today. Max's teacher was so concerned. He gave Max a big hug when we came back to the walk. His teacher is a dad and I can see that he gets it. He tells me that it is just always something. Yup, excellent way to sum up parenthood!

I leave Max and go for lunch, and to get Lillie a very-needed nap. I head back to school holding my breath wondering what Max will be like. Max and Ella head to the playground and Max isn't playing. Now I know it is real that he is truly in pain!

We head home for dinner, and then back to school for the Ice Cream Social/Arts Fest night. The kids are so excited to show me their artwork. I push Max and Lillie in a stroller while Ella tells me it isn't fair that she has to walk. My kids are too much!

Everyone is running up to Max asking him about his foot. News travels fast through school. My friend tells me Max is a celebrity (not how I wanted my child to be a celebrity lol).

We happily head home and I text yell at my husband that he needs to FaceTime his children now! He has been away for days. Ella is having major Daddy withdrawal, and Max wants to make sure he can tell Seth about his day!

The kids are asleep, and I don't think I can go to my bed quick enough. Two more days until Daddy gets home. Here's hoping for a boring, uneventful weekend! Wish me luck!

Max missed his first spring soccer game, baseball practice, a birthday party and a communion party. Max checked out for the weekend. Saturday, he refused to walk despite my telling him his little hole in his foot was not a big deal. I'm such a nice mom! Just trying to calm down my drama king – I mean sweet sensitive boy.

It is Monday and Max asked me to sign him out of gym. I pick him up from school and he is now running on the playground. This from the kid who said he couldn't do gym. Looks like someone is feeling better!

Always eventful! Daddy is home and exhausted from his trip. Maybe, just maybe, a needed break is in sight. I am happy Seth is home, and I am happy Max feels better. Here's to a good calm boring normal week ahead! I can keep hoping for boring! Boring is good!

Lessons:
Hiking boots for the next walk (or better sneakers)! First aid kit necessary!
Take action – protect – be Mama Bear!
Go on field trips!
Stay in shape! You never know when running will come in handy!

BINKIE BEAR

My son was two-and-a-half when I took his binkies away. I told myself I would do the same thing with Lillie. However, it was much harder with my baby. I saw Max's speech changing and I flipped out and took him to Build-A-Bear. He stuffed the dog with his binkies and life moved forward. He had one meltdown on the way home and that was it. Somehow, I knew Lillie would be different!

I passed the two-and-a-half year point with Lillie, and my husband kept asking me when I was taking the binkies away. The pressure! I know he is right, and I know what I said, but she is my baby.

I see Lillie's teeth moving, I see her speech changing, and I know what I have to do!

Seth takes the morning off and we head to Build-A-Bear. Lillie is telling us the whole way there she doesn't want to go. She is holding her bag of binkies like a good girl and isn't opening the bag. I am already impressed with her!

Lillie walked into Build-A-Bear and got very excited to pick something. A bear, a dog, a kitten, a pony...I know this is not going to be an easy decision for a two-year-old to make. Of course, she keeps picking a small bear that she can't stuff. Note to Build-A-Bear: make smaller versions for our little toddlers to be able to stuff!

Lillie thinks she wants a My Little Pony but finally ends up picking out an Elsa bear. The staff at Build-A-Bear are awesome. Lillie runs over with her bear and her binkies ready to stuff the bear. The staff person gets so excited for Lillie and tells her how brave she is. Lillie is beaming with pride. She stuffs the bear with all her binkies and then shows Seth and me her muscles. She gets it! She knows she is being brave and strong!

Lillie holds on to her binkie bear tightly running through the mall. We get to the car and she is whining for a binkie. I tell her to cuddle the bear and we head for lunch. "Mama, binkie, Mama, binkie," she says over and over as I tear up. I look at Seth and he tells me I did the right thing. I am so sad and so thankful my husband came with me. Note to moms – this doesn't faze my husband. I could have sent him with Lillie, and he would be fine. I am the big sap!

We attempt to eat lunch as Lillie lies down on the chairs. Who are we kidding? She is toast and needs to go home to sleep. When we get home, I run through the house looking for binkies and hiding them. Days later I am still finding binkies! The rest of the day flies by. Lillie doesn't ask for her binkie. She goes to bed easily, hanging on to her bear. I am holding my breath because in my heart I know it isn't over.

Lillie asks for her binkie many times. She tells me to put it in her mouth because she knows they are in the bear. The second night she tossed and turned and cried on and off all night. I feel so sad for her. I keep telling myself I did the right thing. My husband and mother tell me I did the right thing. My friends tell me I did the right thing. I am still sad. My baby!

The next two nights she sleeps well! Lillie asks for her binkie, but I say, "You can have a blankie, your baby, your bear or a book." She now has four new B's. I am not turning back. I am still sad for her. I miss comforting her with her binkies.

I don't miss:
Asking her to take her binkie out so I can understand her.
Looking for binkies.
Watching her drag her binkie across the floor and put it in her mouth.

I have gotten through five days! It isn't over but we are making progress. I will give Lillie some time and then we will move on to potty training. Fun fun! Isn't the third one supposed to potty train herself?

Lessons:
Do as a parent what I know is good for my kids, even if it isn't easy!
Give myself positive self-talk: "You did the right thing!"
Follow through!
Be strong!
Seek support!
Cuddle my toddler!

MOTHER'S DAY

I wake up and look at the clock and see that it is 9 a.m. I smile knowing Seth let me sleep in. I wander downstairs and my three kids attack me screaming "Happy Mother's Day!" Max and Ella made me beautiful homemade presents and they are so excited to give them to me!

Seth hands me a box of chocolates and I am perplexed. Max said he wanted to buy me a mom necklace earlier in the week, and Seth quickly told him to be quiet. I was waiting to see this necklace all week! Seth said he forgot about that! Max said he wanted to go buy me a necklace and Seth didn't reinforce it. I am not amused and my mood shifts down. Jewelry will always make me happy! Add in some chocolates and flowers and you're golden with me!

Seth then tells me DiCamillo's, where I wanted breakfast is closed, so I am bummed further. Seth heads to Panera to get us all breakfast and I attempt to relax on the couch.

We eat breakfast and Max completely melts down. His knee is bothering him, and he is on the floor whining and crying. "Hey, it's Mother's Day! Aren't you supposed to behave?" I ask Max. Then I look at Seth pleading for him to deal with Max.

I disappear into the basement to work out and regain some sanity. I am growing annoyed that there is no plan for the day. I am annoyed that there is no necklace. I am annoyed that

Seth isn't handling Max. I know I'm acting like a spoiled brat right now and I better come up with a plan for the day.

My parents bring over a new steam mop for me and I am off the wall excited! I know you are probably confused but I really could use a steam mop. I am super excited to clean my floors. I know, I am nuts!

We get in the car and head to Glen Falls. We pull in and park and it starts raining and thundering. I laugh and quickly get back in the car.

Seth wants to go look at million dollar houses (he dreams big) in the hopes that driving around will get Lillie to take a nap. It sounds good to me, but Max and Ella have a fit, so we go home. I know I shouldn't let them win but I just could not deal with any more complaining.

We watch a Hallmark movie and head to dinner to meet all our parents. Seth's parents are divorced so there are three sets of parents!

We have a nice dinner with our family. Seth's mom and stepdad give me a beautiful card and necklace that says Love. I look at Seth and I know he knows what I am thinking: "You are so lucky Mr. Greene that your mom bought me a beautiful necklace and got you off the hook!"

Seth is determined to take me back to Glen Falls. It is beautiful outside now and we have a nice time with the kids (when we are not protecting Lillie from herself). I got some great pictures and the kids were thrilled to see a ton of ducklings.

I don't dare tell Seth I want to go to Yotality for Frozen yogurt. I can tell he is done, and it is time to go home. It wasn't the day I imagined in my head, but it was surrounded by a ton of love (and chaos). My kids aren't perfect. They cry and whine and complain and have tantrums. Whose children don't? Happy Mother's Day!

My Lessons:
Have no expectations = no disappointment!
Be specific with what I would like to do!
Know that kids will be kids – even on Mother's Day!

ONE BIG HAPPY FAMILY

Whenever I know I need to pack for a trip I tend to do anything else instead. I catch up on laundry and clean my house to avoid packing. I should be jumping to pack because of being excited to take a trip but packing for five people overwhelms me.

On Wednesday night I dive in getting my girls involved in picking outfits to pack. I get all three kids packed and save packing myself for the next day.

It is now Friday morning at 6 a.m. and Seth and I are loading up the car for the long drive. We brought a DVD player for each child and lots of movies. This drive we won't hear them fighting over what movie to watch. Can we say spoiled?

I brought sandwich bags for the treats they picked so I could dump some in a bag from the big box. I brought lots of snacks and books for them to look through. We stop a few times to let the kids stretch their legs.

I think Max asked us every 10 minutes how much longer we would be in the car. It was a long day! Seth has decided that he likes to drive most of the way to avoid waiting on our children. You've heard this before, and it still stands true.

My friend told me to find a Chick-fil-A. Seth and I had stopped at McDonald's for lunch so the kids could play but we couldn't get ourselves to eat. We are almost to my brother's house, but Seth and I are starving so he veers off to get us some Chick-fil-A. I hear a voice calling me in the parking lot and it is my friend from Buffalo who moved to Virginia! It is a small wonderful world!

The kids are thrilled to have arrived. My nephews and sister-in-law are home when we get there, and my parents beat us there. I feel bliss every time I walk through their door. It is one of my very favorite places to be! Thankfully there is room for my party of five and my parents to stay in their house. One big happy crazy family!

We head to a barbeque restaurant and my parents my kids and I attempt to eat the food put out. Seth is easy and eats and doesn't complain. I wish I was easy! The food is too spicy for my kids, my parents and I. We head to a burger place, a cupcake place, and then we all collapse!

It is Saturday morning and the guys are all getting ready for their big day of golf. We are there to celebrate Palmercare's 10th anniversary. A golf tournament and dinner to celebrate an amazing team of people!

My mom and I stay home with all five kiddos and my sister-in-law heads to the golf tournament. The kids play outside for hours and my mom and I enjoy every minute of seeing the cousins play together. My heart is swelling with joy, yet I sniffle thinking I wish this happened more often! "Stay in the moment", I tell myself. A new waterslide and two roller coasters keep the kids occupied for hours and hours. We drag them in to get ready and we are off for the dinner celebration. I make the mistake of packing Ella's Barbie to bring to the dinner. My instincts said to leave her at my brother's house. Listen to your instincts people!

The kids all run around in different directions and the guys arrive from golfing. We listen to my brother's speech as he celebrates 10 years of practice. My brother and sister-in-law are chiropractors who have exploded their business and many others' businesses. My brother, my sister-in-law and my husband have such passion for their businesses. I am in awe of it. Now that I think about it...my parents have a passion for their business and so do I.

1.   My brother and sister-in-law's passion for chiropractic/wellness.
2.   My husband's passion for marketing and business.
3.   My parents' passion for health foods, vitamins and herbs/health.
4.   My passion for marriage and families (social work).

We could build an empire!

We arrive home with the kids and Ella can't find her Barbie! I know I packed it. I run to find the bag. The issue is I never had the bag. My mom and my husband carried my bags for me. I never even checked them. The thought, "I am a terrible mother," runs through my mind as I think about how much my daughter loves her Barbie. She isn't in the bag and I promise to look for her tomorrow.

I wake up and rush to get ready to run over to the country club. My brother drives me, and we can't find this Barbie anywhere. If you saw her, you would laugh. Ella has broken her many times, and Seth and I keep duct taping her back together. I am worried someone thought she was garbage and threw her out! I have bought Ella the same exact Barbie, but she is so attached to the first one. She has dreadlocks and duct tape, but Ella loves her. "Bad mom, bad mom," keeps playing in my mind. Why, oh why am I always so hard on myself?

I brought the exact Barbie with me. I am tempted to have my brother step on her and duct tape her for me. I am tempted to try to pass her off as the real Barbie, but I don't want to lie to my daughter.

I walk in and Ella asks if I found Barbie. My sweet girl is holding back tears as I say no and the tears flow down my face. My sweet sister-in-law Vivian says she is taking Ella to American Girl to buy her a doll to make her feel better. Ella instantly cheers up. She loves American Girl dolls!

We all head to Tysons Corner chaos. Ella gets her doll and I enjoy time with my family despite holding my breath for all the Barbie grief. I am allowing a Barbie to upset me this much. I can't tell you how much I cried over letting this Barbie get lost!

We head home and the kids run to the waterslide. Max and Ella are fighting, but Chase and Ashton are running around so cute together. Lillie goes up and down the roller coaster 50 more times despite the big wound she got from it on her leg yesterday. Somehow her leg got caught. I missed it and my mom doesn't know what happened. I have to realize that sometimes, stuff just happens!

Max comes up to me with tears in his eyes telling me he doesn't want to leave. Ella comes over to me and tells me we can't leave without Barbie. I grab Seth to escape to get gas for our car and allow myself to just be sad. Seth says he cannot believe I am allowing myself to be this sad over a Barbie. "Time to let Barbie go," he tells me.

We go home and play tag and soccer with the kids. I am playing outside with my brother having flashbacks of us as children. We played outside for hours just like my kids love to do.

We head to bed and after Lillie slapping me all night I wake up to Max tapping me at 6 a.m. to tell me he is up. Thanks Max! Max is sad to leave, Ella is sad to leave without Barbie, my dad is crying hugging my brother goodbye, and Lillie tells me she wants to stay at Aunt Vivian's house and doesn't want to leave. Okay, I get it, we are all sad. We love our family and we will make plans to come back soon!

We are on the drive home as I type this. Every so often Ella asks for Barbie and Seth knows to handle it. He knows I am a puddle of mush, and I can't even respond, or I cry. Seth tells

Ella that Grace (new doll) will keep her company. There are moments when I fall even more in love with my husband. This is one of those moments. We are a perfect team!

It is my turn to drive and Lillie is now screaming and melting down. "I want to go to the American Girl doll store right now," Lillie screams at the top of her lungs. "Hold me Mama," she cries. I reassure Lillie several times that I am just looking for a gas station. I tell Lillie I have a surprise in the trunk for her when we get gas. If I stay calm and sweet, she tends to calm down. When I don't have my you-know-what together, she screams louder!

We stop for gas and I get the kids a treat and pull out new Shopkins for Lillie and Ella. A movie and new toys will keep them quiet for a little while.

Long trip tip: bring new toys they don't know about, and new movies they have never seen.

We are 45 minutes from home. We had an eventful weekend. Life with children is never dull! A piece of my heart lives in Virginia. I love my brother and his family dearly. My kids tell me to move to Virginia. They can't understand why we all don't live near each other.

Now wish me luck as I arrive home without Barbie. Happy travels! Happy parenting!

Some lessons:

1) You read my car tips — new movies, new toys, snacks, books!

2) Leave treasured toys at home!

3) Enjoy the present. It is a gift!

4) Visit family often!

5) Remember that you are human. Maybe I can learn to be easier on myself!

6) Celebrate your successes. I am so proud of my brother, sister-in-law, and their whole team!

ERIE COUNTY FAIR

The summer weekends are coming to a close and I want to do a lot of summer fun stuff with my family. Seth suggests Fantasy Island and I suggest the Erie County Fair (it is also the fair's last day). Max is already complaining, saying he needs a place with water and doesn't want to go to the fair. My men don't want to go – that should be my red flag right there. I ignore this red flag and off we go to the fair!

First thing in the door my kids find the toy cart! Lillie grabs a Barbie package – cell phone, jewelry, magic wand, etc. and Max grabs a sword. "Give me strength," I say to myself as I move them into the fair.

Games are everywhere and my kids want to play everything. Seth says "No, no, no, no," and then tells each of them they can play one game! Is he nuts? Has he completely lost his mind? Seth lectures us that he is not spending $24 for a Peppa Pig doll. He is not spending $5 for a dollar store toy. Sometimes it sucks being married to a financial planner, but he is right!

Moving on to the smelly – I mean adorable animals everywhere. My germ phobias kick in and I yell that my kids can't touch anything! Aren't Seth and I so much fun? I think I am funny telling Seth the bunnies are for sale. He is not amused with me!

Max jumps on a very cool trampoline thing and Ella and Lillie go on the carousel. It has only been an hour and a half, and the men are ready to leave. Seth looks done and Max is hanging on me complaining that it is hot. What about shopping? Seth looks at me like I am nuts, but we head to

shopping. (Ella says first I have to tell you that she had to get a funnel cake at Ella's funnel cake stand!)

Ella is such a good kid! I can't express how easy and sweet she is most of the time. She is just going with the flow – easy breezy. "Okay, let's shop," she says. Thank you, Ella. You give me sanity!

Lillie is screaming, refusing to go in the stroller. "Uppy Mommy!" Lillie screams. My back is throbbing, but she is my baby and of course I carry her. I left my baby carrier in the car because I thought she would go in the stroller. My poor back!

I drag my family shopping and Max and Lillie hang on me the entire time. I'm thinking I should just come to the fair with Ella next year. Seth doesn't like anything I pick, and he has this look that says, "When are we leaving?" Fun Family Time!

As I look at the map attempting to head back to the car, Lillie trips and falls and is crying hysterically. Her ankle is hurt from last weekend, her finger is now hurt from this weekend, and I would just like my toddler to slow down. Funny, right? I think I yell "walk" all day long to Lillie as she runs along. My children have developed an amazing skill to tune me out. If only I could develop the skill to tune them out as well as they tune me out!

We make it to the car and Seth looks completely fried. He is miserable and heads to a cold shower as soon as we get home. Ella and I look at each other, thinking at least we had a good time! Happy Family Memories!

My lessons:
Do not bring Seth and Max to the fair next year!
Always remember a carrier for Lillie and always bring bandages!

BACK TO SCHOOL

It has been a great summer! I have enjoyed "Camp Mom." I have had moments of pure insanity where I wanted to run away like every parent, but for the most part I have been having a fabulous time. I am that mom who is sad that summer is ending. It is my favorite time of year! Less than a week of summer left and we will need to get back to a serious routine. I have loved not having a routine but know we will all adjust to having a schedule. I put my kids to bed at 10 o'clock last night because I am in total denial of summer ending. I quickly told them this morning they need to get to bed much earlier tonight. I'd better start tonight! (Okay, maybe.)

I was up all night worrying about my six-year-old. My sweet easy dolly is off to first grade this year. As Max found out about friend after friend in his class, Ella started asking me and worrying who would be in her class. I keep assuring her she has friends in her class, and she has an awesome teacher. I keep assuring her she is the sweetest kid I know, and she will make more new friends. Parenting has made me an amazing actress. I see the worry on her face and I just want to take it away! I was Ella as a kid. I worried and was sweet and sensitive and outgoing just like my girl. I am working on making her childhood easier for her than mine was for me. Don't get me wrong, I had an awesome childhood and I am so blessed. I also had no confidence in myself. I want to instill confidence in my kids at an early age. I want them to take on challenges head-on and know they can do it. I want Ella to march into first grade confident and ready to take it on. "I will create this for my kids!" Let me rephrase that: "I am creating confident children!" This is my mission.

I just told Max that I am so excited for him for third grade. He looks at me and sadly tells me he has already topped out with his last teacher. He is so serious! Max had such an amazing year last year that his expectations are in the toilet. Well let me tell you something Maxwell, "You are eight years old and you have not topped out! You are going to have a ton of teachers and a ton of friends and you have amazing years ahead of you." Max has a fantastic third grade teacher and is with a bunch of his friends. It is going to be a great year, Maxwell. Put on a smile and be excited!

Lillie is begging me to take her to school. Nursery school cannot start soon enough! Lillie has asked me every day for a month when school starts. Lillie will wave goodbye when I take her to class, and she won't look back. (One can hope!)

I wish all of you parents, teachers and children a fabulous school year. I hope they all keep their old friends and make new ones. I hope they all love their teachers and love to learn!

Happy September!

Lessons:
Your kids model you. Show them how easy it is to make a new friend! Show them how to be nice to people! Show them how to start the new school year happy and with confidence! Assure them they can do it!

Get them back on schedule before I do!

CRAZY PUKING SEPTEMBER

It is the day before school starts and Ella spends the day throwing up. I run in another room to cry several times this day. First, Ella is so tiny I can see her ribs. As if I don't worry enough, her thin physique makes me worry more as she pukes all day and can't even keep down a sip of water. Secondly, Ella has been so excited to go to school. Who misses their first day of school? Ella does! Ella spent the first day of school sleeping on the couch. She spent her second day of school home, but at least she was beginning to eat again. I was finally able to send her to school on the third day! I cannot believe this is how September started. I cannot believe the last day of summer ended with puke. Moving on!

First grade is going smoothly. Ella loves her teacher and knows children in her class. I am already hearing about new girls she is becoming friends with. She doesn't know this when she starts first grade, but one of the girls in her first grade class becomes one of her best friends.

Third grade is also going well. Max came home to tell me that his teacher is nice and has a sense of humor. He loves a good sense of humor and loves to laugh. He has a bunch of friends in his class and tells me his favorite part of the day is his gifted and talented math class. Go Max!

Lillie is so excited to start school! She has gotten to go a couple of times and seems to like it. Amazing how we are all back to the routine of going to bed early, getting up early, doing homework and packing lunches.

It is 10:30 and this exhausted mama is about to fall asleep. Lillie starts crying and moaning. I try to think what could have upset her stomach. Seth goes in a second time and then yells as Lillie pukes ALL over the place!

I grab Lillie and throw her in the shower with me. I scrub her and hold her and then comfort her as she throws up all through the night. Every time I begin to fall asleep Lillie throws up again. 5 a.m. it seems to stop. I have become quite an expert in getting my girls to puke in the pot. Target practice as I steer their heads into the pot.

While Lillie takes a few minutes to sleep I grab all the puke-filled laundry and drag it to the mudroom. Seth is gagging and I know I have no choice but to deal with it. I wake up after a couple of hours of sleep to the mudroom and bedroom full of laundry. I also realize I have to get Max and Ella to school. I can push through exhaustion. Do I have a choice?

The kids are off to school, and I begin the many loads while taking care of whiny Lillie. I find the bottom of the sink and floor and then begin to scrub off all the puke. Motherhood!

Seth comes upstairs and finds me looking completely defeated. I may be a stay-at-home mom, but I can't be in three places at once! I am not that good. The tears I am trying to stop roll down my face, as I explain that I can't pick up the kids, and how do I take Ella to theater? Life doesn't stop when a kid is sick! Seth rearranges his schedule to help me. Super-husband to the rescue! Sometimes I just can't do it alone.

I sit here typing this as Lillie sleeps. I can't tell you how many times she puked. I can't tell you how much cleaning I did. I can't tell you how many loads of laundry I did. I can tell you that I survived the lack of sleep, the sick toddler, and the moments of insanity. Tomorrow will be easier.

Feel better Lillie!
Have a healthy school year everyone!

My lessons:
1) We are all stronger than we think. I remind myself of this often.
2) Ask for help!
3) Make your kids take their vitamins! (My parents have an awesome health food store, Marlene and Phil's Vitamin and Herb Center.)
4) Wash hands. Eat fruits and vegetables. Drink grape juice (supposed to prevent the stomach flu)!

MANIC MONDAY MORNING MADNESS

It is Monday morning and Seth is out of town. I have geared myself up for a lot of solo parenting this week. I am on a roll making lunches, feeding the kiddos breakfast and helping them get dressed. I am in the home stretch and am almost to the car to take them to school.

Max grabs his chest and falls to the ground telling me his chest hurts. If this was any other kid, a mom could be upset by this. I tell Max to get his shoes on. He is going to school. It is always something with Max!

Max holds his chest and moans and groans. "My chest, my chest," he is now yelling. I explain to Max that he probably has indigestion from drinking his smoothie too quickly. I hand him water and tell him to try burping. I was almost to the car! I almost had a smooth morning!

Max starts burping and smiling because he is feeling better and thinks burping is hysterical. Eight-year-old boys love burps and farts! Okay, looks like the chest crisis is over.

Max realizes he has nothing in his backpack besides his lunch and snack and starts freaking out that I lost his stuff (agenda, folder, notebook). I calmly tell him he didn't bring anything home. "It is all your fault!" Max yells and starts crying. I am trying to understand how forgetting stuff at school is my fault.

I want to scream. I want to hide and cry, but I gather myself and take a deep breath. If I am calm and sweet, my kids calm down. If I scream and get mad, the situation escalates.

"Max it is okay to forget things. Your teacher and I don't expect you to be perfect and I doubt she gave you homework after your Halloween party." Somehow this came out of me. Sometimes I actually like what I say. It is much better than what I really want to say!

"Okay, but please walk me in and help me talk to my teacher!" Max is holding back a total meltdown. 1) He needs to be able to admit when he does something wrong. 2) He needs to be calmer about things. I have a lot of work to do to teach all this to Max.

I drive the kids to school and walk Max to class. There in his desk are his folder, agenda and notebook. I flip open his agenda to show him he had no homework. His teacher looks at me and I explain the situation. She assures Max he had no homework. Max then proceeds to flip out about his library book, which is there on the floor. He forgot he brought it. Everything is not a big deal! Get me out of here!

Off to get a big coffee even though it should probably be a big glass of wine! Max is a wonderful kid. He is smart and funny and so sweet. Max is also not easy. I am absolutely exhausted and it is only 9 a.m.

THE DRIVE HOME

A 10-minute drive home felt like eternity. My three-year-old tried to grab a mint and my husband grabbed it. I walk over to the car hearing Lillie wailing, wondering what on earth set her off this time. When I discover the problem, I explain that the mint is too big for her and she will choke. I buckle her in while she is screaming and begin to zone out. I know this is going to be a long car ride home. Everything is a big deal when you are three.

Lillie screams and screams. I tell her daddy ate the mint and it is gone. This makes her more upset. Seth tells me he needs some whiskey, trying to laugh about how crazy this whole ride is.

Lillie has now moved from screaming about the mint to screaming about wanting to hear *Uptown Funk*. I can't seem to look at my phone to get it for her because all the stress has made me extremely carsick. "Seth, I need you to pull over. I'm too sick. I will drive and you figure out my phone!"

Seth pulls into a plaza and Max starts asking for Yolicious frozen yogurt. Max and Ella are being so good, but I tell them there is no way Lillie deserves to go there and I need to go home. Lillie is now screaming for frozen yogurt.

Seth gets *Uptown Funk* running and Lillie calms down. We pull in the driveway as Lillie looks like she is falling asleep. Ella tells me Lillie is asleep, but Lillie screams that she is not asleep and wants to drive around. I foolishly get everyone out and begin to pull out, thinking she will go to sleep. She starts screaming that she wants to drive. I can't hear her through the screams. I figure out what she wants, and I tell her she can drive. I put her in the driver seat, and I sit next to her typing. She is giggling and happy. I look over and I realize how short my patience is with her. She is number three. I am tired and I just want her to behave and be easy. I don't want her to scream about everything. Maybe, just maybe, if I am sweeter and more patient, this will go smoother.

Motherhood is quite the interesting journey. It challenges me in capacities I didn't know possible. My children push me over my limits. They make me grow in ways I didn't even know I needed. Just when I think I am patient they show me I am not patient enough. Just when I think I am kind they make me realize I can be kinder. Frustrated, tired, exasperated Mommy is going to be more patient and kinder. Pass me some wine!

I AM CEO

I wake up with a list like this in my mind:
Girl Scouts
PTA
Bowl-A-Thon
Theater
Birthday parties
Max birthday

I jump out of bed knowing I have to get Ella to theater early. I wake up Ella and have a blast doing her hair and makeup. I have the list of requirements: red lipstick, pink blush, purple eyeshadow, tan pantyhose, black shoes, curling iron. The lists in my head tend to be endless! There are lists posted all over my kitchen island.

Ella and I are ready, so I drop her at rehearsal and hand them picture money, DVD money and camp money. I am always writing checks for something! Time to vent all my stress and put myself in a really good state. Workout time, my favorite time!

I drop Ella with her grandmother for a date and run home. Why does it feel like I am always in my minivan? I definitely need a Mommy Taxi sticker on my van!

I have addressed my theater lists and have moved on to birthday parties. Max and I organize three birthday presents and three birthday cards for three of his friends. January seems to be birthday party month!

Seth threw a bunch of stuff at me for a school Bowl-A-Thon basket, so I put that together with a few guidelines from him. The "Grow Your Business" basket is complete, and my parents show up. Max is off to get new roller blades for his birthday and Lillie screams to go with them. Seth and I look at each other in amazement that we are childless, and we soak up some peaceful silence. I know there are many people who don't like silence. I am not one of those people. Silence is golden!

I order a bunch of stuff for Max's birthday party while thinking about the need to book Ella's birthday party. I look at the sink overflowing and the laundry overflowing and the crumbs all over the floor and I start to slip into an overwhelmed tailspin. "It is okay," I tell myself. You are the CEO of the family. You can do all this!"

I update Quicken for my kids' school and begin to work on the school treasurer report for January. For those of you who don't think I have a job, I tend to take on many jobs. I just don't get paid!

I add patches to Ella's Girl Scout vest and Seth gets her cookie account all set online so Ella can sell more Girl Scout cookies.

The kids all come home, and we head off to a skating party. I feel 16 every time I put on roller blades. Now Ella wants a skating party for her birthday. She had a blast, as did Max.

How many parties can one person plan in a year? How many things can a mom balance?

I lie in bed thinking about the day. I think about theater, Girl Scouts, birthday parties, treasurer work, and I tell my brain it is time to rest. I am the CEO! I can handle all of this! I can keep my house and my family running smoothly. I am capable and organized and hardworking. Why do I write this? I write this because instead of stressing or judging others, instead of being sad or overwhelmed, I want you to take a deep breath, give yourself a pat on the back and say "Good job!"

MAX'S BIRTHDAY WEEKEND

I watch Max sitting at the computer giggling away. "What are you reading?" I am very curious. "I am reading your blog Mommy," he tells me! "You haven't written about my birthday," he says, disappointed. "Oh yes I have....."

I pick Max and Ella up at school and we head to the cheesecake place for Max to pick a cake. We head home and get ready to head to Red Lobster with all the grandparents to celebrate Max. My baby is turning nine. It feels like I gave birth to him yesterday. I remember so many details of that day. I remember bringing him home with snow falling. I keep tearing up thinking about it. It truly goes so fast!

Max gets lobster, and then begins to try to lie on me at the restaurant. He is full and whiny and I am fighting major exhaustion. Heading home can't happen soon enough for me! Despite us warning Max to behave at the restaurant, he usually ends up attempting to lie down saying he is tired. It never fails!

We wake up on Saturday and Ella is off-the-wall excited for her first theatre performances! All Ella wants to do is be on stage. Watching Ella on stage is one of my very favorite things! I have a feeling this is the beginning of watching many shows. Max is totally jealous and wants the whole weekend to be about him. Siblings! Seth heads to soccer with Max, and I take Lillie to Ella's performance.

By the time I get there I want to cry. I am emotional about Ella going on stage, I am emotional about Max turning nine, and I am emotional because I desperately need a break. Who scheduled this crazy weekend? Oh yeah, that would be me. Oops!

The 2:00 performance is over. Ella was fantastic. We go home to rest before the 7:00 performance. Seth and I decide to drag Max to that show. As a parent, I try to make the best parenting decisions. I ask myself, "Am I making the right decision?" as Max complains about going. The fact is, there isn't always a right decision. What I want to do is drop Max and Lillie at my parents' house to make my life easier. What I end up doing is making Max come to make Ella happy. How many of Max's baseball and soccer games has Ella watched? I need to teach sibling support.

We celebrate at Yotality and head to get Lillie. I put my kids to bed as fast as I can because now is time to get Max's birthday scavenger hunt ready and blow up balloons and put up decorations.

Note to all you parent's out there: once you start something it is hard to stop. When Max was younger, he woke up having to do a scavenger hunt through our house to find his birthday present. Now my kids want this for everything. Birthdays, Valentine's Day, you name it, they ask for a scavenger hunt! Who knew this would be such a hit?

Max wakes up to his scavenger hunt and then begs to go sledding. I am cold already thinking about it and Seth is getting over a cold. Not what either of us wants to do but we drag ourselves sledding. My parents show up and Max shows off his moves on his new snowboard. He would stay all day if I let him!

We head for lunch and then I am off to Wegmans for yet another birthday cake. In the end Max will have had three birthday cakes. What on earth am I thinking? Sometimes I actually want to slap myself. Max does not need three birthday cakes.

Time for the school Bowl-A-Thon. Max has an absolute blast bowling all night. A crazy fun time with friends everywhere and Max is in his glory! My sentimental boy is a sad mess going home, knowing his birthday is ending. I reassure him that next weekend is going to be awesome. An American Ninja Warrior birthday party coming his way! He goes to bed sad and wakes up crying. "My weekend was so amazing. I didn't want it to end!" I keep reminding him it isn't over.
"Can we go sledding again?"
"Can we go bowling again?"
"Can we do another scavenger hunt?"
I try to be as sweet as I can, but I am absolutely exhausted because Lillie had a really bad night sleep and kept me up.

I get through Monday and I give myself a pep talk. One more crazy weekend, and then life is going to calm down. I can hope!

THE BIRTHDAY CONTINUES

Earlier you read about Max's fun-filled birthday weekend last weekend. This weekend it was time for more fun! Someone thought it was a good idea to schedule a bunch of things during our weekend again. Someone thinks we are Energizer bunnies. Yes, I know, "What was I thinking?" I ask myself that question regularly!

Let's begin our weekend by taking our kids to *Disney On Ice*. I was done after that. I was ready for a nap. I talked myself into being a good mom and going to watch Max's soccer game. Why don't I give myself permission to rest? Why didn't I lie down and cuddle the girls at home? There will be a ton of soccer games to watch. I push myself and go to the game. "It is okay to stay home and rest," I tell myself as a mental note for another time. I am a better mom when I am well-rested. I really do love watching Max play soccer, and I never want to miss it if I don't have to.

We come home from soccer and I help Ella get ready for her dance. Seth and Ella are going off to the Girl Scout father-daughter dance. I watch them leave and my eyes fill with tears. I know my husband and I know this is a dream come true for him. I love how Ella loves her daddy! It is so precious!

Lillie is at my parents' house, and Max and I head to meet friends at Dave and Busters. I would call that place a "kids' casino." Max has a blast, and I leave happy, tired, and with a headache. Do any parents leave Dave and Busters happy?

I go to bed thinking I cannot believe Max's party is tomorrow. I cannot believe that his birthday stuff isn't over. Please let it be over!

I get everything organized for the party and hope I am remembering everything.

Things to remember:
Plates
Napkins
Candles
Lighter
Knife
Spatula
Waters
Favors
Scissors to cut Ella's pizza

I get a few texts from friends. One is telling me she decided they aren't coming. Her daughter had the stomach flu badly and she doesn't want to bring any potential germs from her, her son, or her daughter. Can I tell you how thoughtful this is? Can I tell you how much I love and appreciate this friend? We missed them but that was very sweet of her. Thank you, friend!

We load up the car and are on our way downtown. I hate going downtown. Did I mention Seth and I booked a party at a place where we've never been? This is the second time I've done this. The first time worked out. Let's hope I am two for two! Let's just say I am pretty nervous.

The only thing Max wanted for his birthday was an American Ninja warrior party. Seth and Max watch the TV show and Max is so excited to have an American Ninja warrior birthday party (and so is Seth)! Is the party for my son or my husband?

We find the place and meet the owner. So far so good. The place isn't big like I pictured but is very cool. They are going to organize stations for the kids to do. Where is the party room? The owner assures us the kids will eat on the floor, and it will go well, and he does a ton of birthday parties. Okay, let's take his word for it.

I say a prayer for all the kids to be safe (no accidents on my watch please), and the party runs smoothly. They have the kids running through stations for an hour and everyone seems to be having a fabulous time. Seth even got one of the dads to join in with him. I see Seth and Max trying one thing after another and I smile. My men are so happy! Not just my men though. I look over and see Ella and Lillie trying everything too. My whole family is happy, and their friends are happy too. This feeling is amazing! Can I bottle it and save this feeling for many hours (instead of just the hour-and-a-half party)? Let's not discuss what we paid for this hour-and-a-half party. Let's keep the total spent out of my husband's earshot!

The kids have pizza and chicken fingers and then dive into the magnificent American Ninja Warrior cake that my friend made for Max. Is it really over?! How does it go so fast? An hour and a half is too short for a birthday party!

Everything is dragged home and Max dives into all the generous thoughtful presents. Minecraft, nerf guns, soccer ball, football, gift cards, games. All I can say is Max is one lucky kid! Thank you, friends! Thank you for celebrating with Max, thank you for the generous gifts, thank you for being such great friends! Let's not forget the amazing grandparents! They are at every event. Soccer, theatre, baseball, birthdays, you name it, they are there to see us and be supportive.

We clean up the big giant mess and organize his presents (mostly), and now I see we have to get ready for our friends' birthday party. Yes, I know. My family and everyone else thinks I am crazy right now. I do too! Ella and Lillie are excited to go swimming and see our friends. Max is toast. He wants to go to my parents and rest, but Seth makes him come with us. Note to self: it is okay to overrule my husband when I think he is wrong. Max needed to rest. Yes, sometimes my amazing, wonderful husband is wrong!

We head to the Y and get our kids dressed for the pool. They swim and have a blast and then Max is ready to go home and crash. My friend puts out a nice spread of food and the girls are perfectly easy and content. Max is moping and wanting to leave. Max is at that place: That place of no return. That place of driving me completely nuts! Why did we bring him? Oh yes, thank you Seth!

The weekend ends, and I am tired, but I feel so thankful! I spent too much money (so sorry honey) but we had a blast. My son had an amazing party and we saw so many friends and family members this weekend. I absolutely love going to *Disney On Ice*. Forget the kids, I want to go for me! Feeling tired but feeling blessed. (Also feeling happy that I have zero scheduled tomorrow!) Seth will be running to work to get a break!

ELLA'S BIRTHDAY

I certainly can't write about Max's birthday without writing about Ella's. At this point my kids ask me to write about certain things, which melts my heart. My sweet Ella turned Seven! My middle child who wants everyone to get along. The one who interferes when Seth and I are fighting to say something so smart like "You guys are the best couple." She is a natural therapist! We can't help but stop fighting and look at each other with a big smile. Ella is the child who sees my stress and tells me what a good job I am doing as her mom. She lights up the room and really helps to keep me sane every day!

If Ella wants something it is really hard to say no to her. She told Seth and me:

1) She wants to go to Panera for her birthday dinner with her grandparents and parents and siblings. She wouldn't listen to any other restaurant suggestions. She didn't want me to make anything. She only wanted Panera!

2) She was in a theatre performance that talked about boogie shoes and a roller rink. All she wanted to do was have her birthday party at a roller rink. Shout out to the *Academy of Theatre Arts* for a great performance! "Ella, don't you think first graders will have trouble skating? What about a girls' spa party?" I'm trying to entice her. "No way Mom, I want a roller rink with my whole class. I want to put on my boogie shoes!" How do I say no to her?

3) Can she please get an iPad? You may think Seth and I are totally nuts. I get that. However, Max has an iPad and then Lillie tends to use Seth's, which means Ella ends up without one. With the help of all the grandparents we bought Ella an older version of a mini iPad. Totally spoiled children! I am very guilty. For the record, I do not even have an iPad!

It is Ella's birthday morning and I am hustling like I am every morning to get everyone ready, but Ella is begging for her scavenger hunt. We do a scavenger hunt on every birthday. It has become tradition. If I try to skip it, they get upset, so I will humor them and keep doing scavenger hunts. Note to self: do scavenger hunts after school. They do the hunt, find their toys, and then want to open and play with these toys! "I can't take it," I yell. I am trying to get them ready and they are asking me to open things. Now Ella is looking at me with sad eyes. No, no, no.....I can't have her upset on her birthday! "I am so sorry Ella! I am sorry I yelled. I just want you happy on your birthday. I learned today that scavenger hunts have to happen after school. You can play with your stuff after school. I have to get you ready for school." She nods and understands, and I get them out the door.

I head to my friend, the lunch lady's house to give her cupcakes so she can give one to Ella during lunch. I love to stop in on their birthdays with a cupcake during lunch, but I was heading to a funeral and my sweet friend was willing to help me. Ella was so excited that my friend turned off the lights during lunch and the cafeteria sang to her! Sometimes in life you click with someone and see their sweet soul shining through. This woman is one of those people in my life. If you read this, a big thank you to you! XO

The brother of one of my best friends died so I head to his funeral. This friend actually came to my grandmother's funeral on her birthday. How can I be so sad and so happy on the same day? I say goodbye to my friend's brother and wish him peace, which he deserves more than anyone, with all he went through. It is so hard to see my friend and her family sad. Now it's time to head to school to read to Ella's class and put a smile back on my face!

I can't tell you how much I love volunteering at my kids' school. My husband and I joke that I should just work there! I tend to take on a lot of volunteer jobs and don't get paid for anything. My husband is a saint for putting up with this. He even gets suckered into helping me with my volunteer jobs because he is such a good guy. I notice and appreciate this Seth!

We head home and the kids happily play with their new toys. I get all of them a little something for every kid's birthday. I want them all to find something at the end of the hunt. I am good at finding ways to spend money. My husband (the one who doesn't want them eating candy) asked me to have candy at the end of the hunt. I refuse to do candy as I am on a mission to buy less and less junk. I am currently doing zero junk food for me. Now to work on my children!

I learned a lesson after Max's birthday. Max had: 1) His actual birthday where we celebrated. 2) A grandparent celebration with all of us. 3) A kid birthday party. I don't want to do three different days if I can help it, so we invited the grandparents to Panera. Let's do the family celebration on Ella's actual birthday and cut out a day for me! Everyone seemed happy with this.

Ella eats dinner, eats cake and goes to open her present. I tell her, "This present is very special. All your grandparents and your parents put their money together to buy you this!" Ella's eyes widen and Max says "I bet it's an iPad!" Did he really just say that? I grab Max and bring him over to me praying Ella barely heard him. Max sees the steam coming out of my ears. He knows when I am really angry and he is playing it down like, "What did I do? It isn't a big deal." He is attempting to calm me down. That kid!

Ella is thrilled and I smile knowing she had a really great birthday. Part of me truly wishes that could be it. Why do we have to have a kid party? Ella, I will re-energize and enjoy your party with you!

P.S. Ella is now obsessed with texting. If she texts you 50 times a day, I am so sorry!! I am much more amused than Seth is.

ELLA KNOWS HOW TO PARTY

As you know from the last chapter, Ella decided she had to have her birthday party at a roller rink. I was a little nervous that the first graders would be falling all over and struggling but I decided all I could do at this point was hope for the best.

Ella asked for a *Descendants* cake, so I had ordered it from my friend. I give her a theme and a flavor and then I let her do her thing. Look how awesome this cake is!

Going with the *Descendants* theme I decided I was going to make favors. I went from necklaces to bracelets to bagging it. There wasn't *Descendants* stuff anywhere and I didn't want to order stuff online and wait. I love Etsy, but when I order stuff  there it takes forever to arrive, and that drives me crazy!

After going back and forth with Ella we decide on a roller theme – Rolos, rollups, Tootsie Rolls and a mini skateboard....a bunch of junk that I shouldn't be feeding the kids! Next time I will stick to necklaces and key chains. Favors are a pain in the you-know-what!

We arrive to the rink, and Ella and Max get their skates on as soon as they can and are off skating! I brought Lillie a scooter and get her started and she is off. All I want to do is put on my rollerblades and go, but I am nice, and I greet everyone. Ella's friends come pouring in and her face is glowing.

If I forgot to invite anyone I apologize. If you know me, you know I want to invite the whole world. However, inviting the whole class kind of did me in.

Seth and I paid a lot to rent out the rink, but Max bugs me the entire night to give him money for the arcade. The kid is arcade obsessed! I must have said "Go skate" to Max 50 times that night!

Seth looks at me dealing with Max and talking to all the moms and says to me, "Go skate!" He is right! He knows I love to rollerblade, so I put them on and attempt to skate. Every time I try, the roller rink employees are asking me questions or Lillie is crying. Lillie clearly does not want me skating and keeps asking me to take my skates off. Motherhood! Note to self – I need to come skate without my children!

Max and Lillie are stressing me out and then I look over at Ella and I see her giggling and skating with her friends, and I feel my reset button get pushed. This is what tonight is about! Ella's friends are all giggling and skating too. These first graders were doing awesome. I was so happy, but then I saw a girl crying trying to skate with her mom, and I run over. I am both a mother and social worker at heart and I never want to see a child upset. When I see how upset this little girl is trying to skate, I run and get Ella's scooter. I am so thankful right now that I brought it. Problem solved – phew! My goal at birthday parties is for all the kiddos to be happy and safe. I do my best!

Ashley arrives with the cake and I am completely amazed! It doesn't matter how many cakes she makes me they get better each time. Ella and I are blown away! We absolutely love this friend so having her make Ella's cake was so special to us.

Pizza (I am so tired of looking at pizza), cake and more skating. I feel myself starting to release the breath that I was holding. Why do I let myself get so stressed? Everything usually works out. Did I mention that I started a cleanse? No gluten, no sugar, no dairy...do you know what this means? No pizza and no cake for this mama. Can we say, "Holy self-control"? I did it! It wasn't easy but I did it. The bottom line is we can all do anything we set our minds on!

While I got to see my kids and their friends having fun, I think the best part was seeing the moms and dads put on skates and have fun. Everyone was telling me this was reminding me of their childhood. Can you guess where I decided to have my 40th birthday? I will be back to party!

We pack everything up and head home. I wanted the party Saturday night, but it was booked, so I did Sunday (a school night)! Ella begins ripping open presents and losing cards. This drive me nuts! I attempt to slow her and Lillie down more times than I can count. It is late. It is a school night. My house is a disaster. *Descendants* dolls and accessories, Shopkins, jewelry, arts and crafts, games, etc. thrown all over the family room. You can guess how happy I am! We get the kids to bed and Seth looks at me with confusion. "You do this to yourself every party," he says looking around the mess of a family room. "Next party all the presents go in the dining room and I will bring one at a time into the family room to open." Yup! He is attempting to solve my problem as he always does. Men love to solve problems. They don't want to hear you complain, they don't want to hear why it won't work. They just want to solve the problem!

The house is somewhat cleaned up and I sit and think about the night. Ella got to put on her boogie shoes and have a great party. She invited her whole class like she wanted, and she got to have it at a roller rink. Mission accomplished! On to planning the next party.

Party on!

MAKE IT STOP

I like to pray. It gives me peace and calms my nerves. When planning a big event, I tend to say prayers about my family being healthy. "Let my three children be healthy and be able to enjoy Ella's party," I prayed many times. Let's get through the party. Well, I didn't say anything about after the party!

Every day I am hearing, "This one has the flu, this one has an ear infection, this one has strep, and this one has the stomach flu." It was making me crazy! I heard that grape juice prevents the stomach flu. My kids' doctor thought I was nuts when I asked her about this. However, guess who hates juice, and guess who got the stomach flu?

Ella comes downstairs and says she is going to sleep on the couch. She says she isn't up for school and asks me if she can stay home. Why on a Tuesday? I was going to drop Lillie at preschool and get a ton of errands done by myself. I was going to go to the gym by myself. Lillie only goes to school Tuesday and Thursday mornings. My sacred time to myself! Ella never asks to stay home so I say okay, and Max and Seth leave. As Seth pulls out of the driveway the puke begins, and she continues the rest of the day! Seth comes home and looks at me and knows to calm me down. "She will be fine," he says to me several times. When Ella gets this sick it is hard for me. She is my super skinny kid. She can't afford to lose weight!

The next day is no better. I have never seen a kid puke this much in my lifetime. Just make it stop! She is begging me for water but throws up every time she takes a sip. My dad does research and finds out to give the body time after you puke (20ish minutes), do a sip of water and sit up. This is supposed to help. My poor baby! Ella is home the rest of the week because two days of puking knocked her out. I am stuck home for days completely going stir crazy. I am not one to stay home.

Saturday Ella is bouncing around and I can't stop smiling. I love seeing my peppy girl back, but Lillie is climbing all over me sneezing and coughing. "No!"

Saturday night Lillie gets a fever. Make it stop! Now Max and I are stuffed up and Seth is leaving on a business trip! How am I going to do this? I remind myself that my parents will help me. I remind myself that I have friends who will help me. I have trouble asking for help. This is something I want you to all get over if you have the same problem. We are just one person. We can't do everything! Three kids tends to equal three different directions. It takes a village!

I am stuffed up and sneezing, I am worn out, but we are on an upswing. We had such a great winter. The cold weather must freeze germs. Warmer weather has not been my friend.

Get sleep!
Take vitamins!
Eat healthy!
And ask for help!

SUNDAY FUNDAY

It is Sunday morning and Hebrew school is cancelled because of Passover. I am thrilled I can relax and make the girls pancakes (that I can't eat). I am losing weight and am doing a fasting day. You can imagine the happy mood I am in today!

I feed the girls while Seth goes to grab Max from a sleepover. Seth and I discussed taking the kids to a newer playground that he wanted to see. Max comes home and gets settled on the couch. I am getting the girls dressed while Max moans that he wants to stay home and relax. Oh please, can I stay home all day with three children and attempt to do nothing? Do you know what that would look like? Let's just say not pretty! Getting out of the house tends to help to keep me sane but I am slowly seeing that Max is not caring much about my sanity today.

The girls are excited to go to the playground, but Max complains the whole way to the car. He wants a pajama day at home, he says to me many times. I guess somehow Max thought he was in charge of our plans for today.

We begin the "long" drive and Max quickly complains that he is carsick. We are driving downtown (which I hate) and we miss our turn to the Skyway (which I do all the time). Seth takes a couple turns and finds another Skyway entrance. We are almost there, and Max is moaning and groaning that he needs to get out of the car. I already have to pee but remember that this playground has an actual bathroom. Do I always have to pee?

The kids get out of the car and the girls quickly head back to the car for their jackets. I am totally freezing (high 50's today) and Max is off in shorts and short sleeves telling me he doesn't want a jacket. Kids! I quickly learn the bathroom is closed for construction. I refuse to use the Porta-Potty. This should be fun. I should be used to holding my pee!

The kids play on the playground and Lillie is having a ball. Max and Ella are quickly bored as Lillie squeals in delight. Seth starts giving Max and Ella ninja challenges to accomplish. I decide I can't hold my pee anymore and we head to Tim Hortons at Canalside for my needed coffee and bathroom! I promise the kids ice cream at our next stop.

At this point I am driving but I can't find parking and am starting to wonder how long I can hold it. Giving birth to three kids definitely affected my bladder. If I laugh too hard, I pee! If I sneeze too hard, I pee! I can thank Max for the three hours of trying to push him out of me. Seth knows me pretty well and drops the kids and me at Tim Hortons and goes to find parking. He knows I am about to lose it and wants to avoid the meltdown. Every child decides to use the bathroom and then wants to order food. I told them they could have donuts or ice cream and they all pick ice cream. I buy my coffee and as we go to leave, Max decides he wants a donut. He then proceeds to start crying as we walk to the ice cream shop telling me how starving he is. Remember, I am fasting today and haven't eaten yet. I have fed Max a couple times already today. He doesn't know what starving is! I am hungry and grumpy and not amused with him. The ice cream place is closed, so we turn around to get donuts. At this point I am laughing, and Max is crying. The girls are going with the flow and Max is crying that he just wanted to have time at home today. I tell Max he is done with sleepovers and he looks at me like I am insane. I explain to Max as calmly as I can at this point that he can only go to sleepovers if he promises not to be cranky the next day. He quickly decides to be happy and devours his donut.

Max asks me what we are doing next. I tell him that I thought we would drive to Rochester and check out a mall there. He thinks I am hysterical and asks where we are really going. "Home!" Seth says with force. So much for Sunday Fun Day! We tried. Points to Seth for coming up with the plan for today. Time to go home!

MOMMY TAXI

I wake up grumpy (never a good sign) and stomp downstairs. I see Max and Seth on the couch and start making lunches. I know Seth is leaving for Denver today. I know I tend to be grumpy when I know he is leaving. I seem to turn to being grumpy instead of being sad. Grumpy is easier for me than sadness. I hate being grumpy, but I hate being sad even more.

Ella and Lillie come down and I continue to work on getting everyone ready. Lunches packed, bags packed, breakfasts eaten (except Lillie, who is fighting me). All the kids are dressed, and I am watching the clock go very quickly this morning. I need to get everyone into my minivan by 8:40 a.m. It is not looking so good!

I rush everyone along and Lillie asks me for breakfast in the car. I get everyone in the car, Seth grabs his suitcase and their backpacks, and we are off. First stop is to drop Max and Ella at school. We pull up to drop them at 8:53 and hope they aren't going to be late. It is at this point I realize I forgot Lillie's breakfast! Now what? The only food in the car I can find is cookies, so that is what

she will get. All I can say is, "third child!" Do you think I would have let my first child eat cookies for breakfast? Next stop is the airport. I really need to buy myself a Mommy Taxi magnet for my car. I am in my car way too much! I drop Seth at the airport and give him a kiss goodbye. I am sad every time he leaves but I know how much his trips help him and our family. I am late so I rush to nursery school and drop Lillie off. I get back into my car at 9:40. It took me an hour to drop everyone off. I laugh and head to the Y to work out. Time for some "me time." I am smiling, knowing I have a couple hours to myself. However, by the time I get there and work out, I have to turn around to pick up Lillie and her friend. Where did the morning go? Why does it go so fast?

I pick up Lillie and her friend and drop the friend off. I run home to feed us, and then run to school to handle some treasury items (I am PTA Treasurer). Just add it to my list. I help with Girl Scouts. I help with softball. I help with the PTA. When do I not help? It is just in my nature. I can't help myself!

With Seth away, I drop Max and Lillie at my parents' house and Ella, my dad and I head to softball. I may be able to help coach, but my dad is the expert. He played and coached baseball forever. He is excited that Ella is playing. Ella has a great practice and turns to me and tells me she loves it and wants to play again next year. All the running around... all the money I spent on the bat, the mitt, the helmet, the clothes... all the softball practices. That smile and happiness beaming from Ella makes it all worth it!

We drop off Ella's friend and run to get Max and Lillie. We run home to shower everyone and deal with homework. If I was a teacher, I would give minimal homework. Come on, it's spring. Let's be done with homework!

How much time did I spend in my car today? I don't want to know. It is just part of motherhood!

Now it is time to put the kids to bed. I want you all to know how much better I feel venting all this. We have to vent! We have to learn to cope! Whether I am screaming to my friends, my mom, my husband, working out or writing, I find ways to de-stress. Motherhood is an amazing joy! My kids are wonderful exhausting little people!

PARENTING THREE VERY DIFFERENT KIDS!

I am that person who loves babies and kids. I am that person who would probably just keep having babies. My husband was good with two kids. I begged him for a third! Seth is made for me in every way. I get frustrated with him when he says he was good with two – but he is here to protect me from myself. How much work do I think I can handle? Am I trying to test my limits? I will admit, I get sad about my baby, who is now three, being so big, and I have many moments of wanting another. I will also tell you, Lillie has been very good birth control! Let's be honest here – if Seth said, "Let's have a fourth," you all know I would say YES!

Max just turned nine years old. He was high energy from the time he was born. I had trouble keeping up with him and knew he needed a ton of stimulation. Max is so smart and ate up everything I taught him. Numbers, letters, colors, shapes, he went into three-year-old preschool knowing all of it. I couldn't imagine what they were going to teach him! I was frustrated at the time but looking back Max needed to learn how to be in school. How to take turns. How to share. How to stand in a line. How to listen to your teacher reading a story. I quickly learned that consequences did nothing to change Max's behavior. I was frustrated until I started to think about what worked. Positive praise and incentives work with Max.

Max is incentive driven. Give him a prize to earn and he will work.

Just when you figure out your first, your next child comes out, and she is completely different!

Seth begged me for number two. I had this sweet mama's boy who always wanted to cuddle his mama. I was content and busy. Max kept me on my toes. Seth was longing for the daddy's girl he had been dreaming of. Well, guess who came next? Sweet Ella, who adores her daddy! I didn't believe them when they told me I was having a girl. I thought for sure I would end up with three boys. They were right. Ella came out sweet and wanting to cuddle and be held. I kept Ella in a baby carrier most of the time because she wanted to be close to me. I nursed Ella forever. Okay, it wasn't forever but it felt long to me! Ella is my sweet easy middle child. She is the child I have to remind myself to give attention to because she doesn't demand it. Ella made me want more children. I can't really tell you the last time I disciplined Ella. At seven years old she is getting a bit of an attitude, but she is my sweet girl!

I begged for Lillie. I worked on Seth for a long time. He reminds me regularly how much I begged for Lillie. My warning to all of you reading this: once you have a baby your body seems to very easily know how to get pregnant again. Let's just say Ella and Lillie came before we had planned!

I could write pages and pages about my third child. After hearing for years that Max and Ella look like Seth, it is truly a special feeling to hear people tell me that Lillie looks just like me. Finally! I could never wrap my mind around how I did all the work and Max and Ella came out looking like Seth!

Lillie is a force of nature. Lillie is fierce and independent. One minute she is throwing something at me and the next minute she is hugging me so tight I can't breathe. I remind myself every day that she loves me dearly. I remind myself every day that her strong independent personality will serve her. She wants to do everything by herself. Max and Ella have always asked for help. This one is so totally different I am back at square one.

It doesn't matter how many kids you parent, every child is different and as their parents we have to figure out what works with them. I have to stay so calm and sweet and patient to get anywhere with Lillie. I fail daily. I end up yelling and/or hurrying her on a daily basis. You would think I would give myself more time to leave the house knowing she will want to do her own coat and shoes. You would think I would take deep breaths and be patient when she is refusing to listen. I try! On a daily basis I "start over" and remind myself who Lillie is and what she needs from me. If I give Ella a mad look, she does exactly what she knows I need her to do. If I give Lillie a mad look, she gives me a madder look back. You know what? Good for Lillie! My strong-willed child. I hope you fly far, and I hope I survive the ride!

For Ella: these are things I needed to be taught as a child. It is most important to please yourself. Stop worrying what other people think! Stand up for yourself! Have a voice! I consistently work on giving Ella what I wish I had as a child. When I saw a child push her out of her chair and Ella did nothing, I was all over that! My sweet girl is sandwiched between a brother and a sister who I have a feeling will not let her get pushed around. My wish for Ella is for me to help give her a voice that took me 30 years to find.

So, there you have it: three very different kids! My advice to myself and all of you is to remember that every child is truly different and deserves for us to figure out how they need to be parented. Wish me luck, I am off to deal with the strong-willed three-year-old!

THE THRASHING THREES

There have been many days when I have "diagnosed" my three-year-old as bipolar. You can't really diagnose a three-year-old that way, but I laugh out loud when I think it. The constant major mood swings can actually be amusing if you decide to look at it that way. Every thought we put into our head is how we have decided to perceive the situation. There have been days I have thought about how much "easier" it would be to head off to work every day and get space from Lillie. Then Lillie looks at me with adoring eyes and gives me a great big Lillie hug and tells me how much she loves me. "You are the best mommy!" she tells me with loving eyes. I tell myself to savor this moment and put it in a box in my mind. I will remember this moment when she is having a tantrum on the floor!

I hear Lillie wake up on the monitor and I feel myself hold my breath. I am hoping that happy Lillie is awakening. You never know how Lillie will wake up. She smiles and says "Hi Mama. What are we doing today?" That may seem so minor to you, but to me that is the pressure sentence. What amazing plans do I have for Lillie today? I don't want to disappoint my child. I love having fun with her. I love taking her places and seeing friends. We also all know that the errands don't do themselves and the house doesn't magically take care of itself. Let's not talk about the endless amounts of laundry that five people create for me. I tell Lillie I have to get some errands done and that she can be my special helper. She is less than amused. She wants to hear me tell her we are going to the zoo or ballet or something she has labeled fun for her. When did it get harder? She used to be amused by going to Target with me. She used to love going to Wegmans with me. What happened? They age out of errands and I have now arrived to that place with all my children.

Seth, Max and Ella head out the door and I battle Lillie to get dressed and out the door. I learned quickly that if I involve Ella and Lillie in the outfit decision-making process, they are much more cooperative in getting dressed. My son Max could care less what he wears and just wants comfy shorts and a t-shirt to throw on and head to school.

Lillie whines in the car that she doesn't want to go to Wegmans and Target. Why do we have mommy guilt? "Can't someone babysit me? I don't want to go with you?" I am sad that she doesn't want to go with me and feel badly that I am dragging her around with me. I reassure myself that I will play with her when we get home and that it is okay to get things done. I can't snap my fingers and get the food and supplies I need, even though that would be an awesome mama superpower to have!

We walk into Target and Lillie screams at the top of her lungs that she wants to go to the toy section. When I had Max that would have embarrassed me. By child #3 I am actually floored if someone gives me a look. "Don't you know what toddlers are like?" is the thought that now runs through my head at a store. I used to run out of the store with Max. I think back to that and laugh at myself and at Lillie who is now screaming at me to put her in the back of the cart. I ask Lillie to use "please" and put her in the cart. The goal is to raise nice polite children. Trust me when I tell you I work hard on this goal!

I grab some of the stuff on my list ignoring Lillie's constant demand for the toy section. I finally reassure her we are heading there, but she is just looking today. For those of you who have been to my house, you have seen the big bins of toys. We have enough! We don't need to add to the mess we already have flowing at home. Lillie is loving every Baby Alive doll and baby she finds. She is eyeing the shelf full of new Shopkins. We don't need any more, they are all over my house. My Little Ponies, princesses, makeup, Play-Doh.....get me out of the toy section without buying anything!

We escape Target and head to Wegmans. Lillie cries when I get to the parking lot. I actually consider going home but why would I give her that much control? Who is in charge? Don't laugh, I know what you are all thinking!

One of our neighbors works at Wegmans and comes over to say hello and give Lillie a banana. Good, a banana will keep her happy for five minutes. Oh wait, I don't want to distract and please her with food. Not the lesson I want her to learn. It is amazing how we mothers use food as a distraction. A cookie, a bowl of goldfish, whatever it takes to keep them quiet and happy. Can we say "survival?"

I am a Wegmans pro (unless they decide to move things) and I fly through the store at super mommy speed as Lillie begs to get out of the cart. I almost made it out in super speed. "Why am I always in a hurry?" I ask myself.

The biggest lesson I have learned as a parent is to PICK MY BATTLES! I do not have enough strength to argue with everyone, and everything isn't worth arguing about. Lillie slows me down when she's out of the cart, but I amuse her and let her walk down the aisles. "I want to walk. I want to buckle myself. I want a cookie. I want another cookie. I want to put the food on the belt. I want to sign for you. I want I want I want." There is very little silence in my life. I tell myself, "Embrace it. Enjoy it. She will be in kindergarten before you blink."

By the time I get home and unpacked I am dripping sweat and exhausted. Lillie is also pooped. She and I cuddle to read books. She throws the book at me and my blood boils. "Breathe, just breathe," I tell myself. This is a battle to pick! Safety comes first, and she decked me with a book. I scoop her up and drag her to time-out. She absolutely freaks out when I take her to time-out. I'm actually glad she doesn't like it. That means it is an effective consequence. Let's just say this is not the only time that she was in time-out today. By the time Seth comes home from work daily he sees the Lillie exhaustion all over me. I work so hard to be calm all day. When I am calm and sweet it goes so much better. We all know this is not an easy task!

Seth is very protective, and when Lillie is mean to me or Max or Ella, he loses it. He walks through the door in his power suit and tie, and I feel the mighty Seth walk through the door. I see how he is standing and looking at Lillie having a tantrum, and I signal to him with my eyes to stay calm. I know he wants to yell at her. I can tell by his stance. He usually can read my face. I love my husband with my whole heart, and I know he just wants Lillie to behave. "She is three," I tell him over and over. "Pick your battles," as I see him begin to fight with Lillie over wearing the right shoes. Seriously? I can't take another Lillie meltdown. "This is why I go to work," he tells me, as if I don't know this.

We sit down at 10:00 at night and debrief. Seth looks at me and he knows it isn't working. He knows the social worker hat is on his wife, and we are about to have a counseling session.

Seth tends to be the strict one and I tend to be the soft one. The saying, "Wait till your father gets home," definitely applies to my family. However, I know better! I know kids need a ton of love and attention, but they also need discipline. I also know the power of our words. Seth and I start to process all the things we say to ourselves and to Lillie:

She is so hard.
The three's suck! Can we get to the four's?
Lillie is a brat.
Lillie doesn't share.
Lillie isn't nice to me.
We are sending negative messages into the universe and to Lillie. Time to change! Seth and I agree to give Lillie and the world a positive message:
Lillie is so sweet.
Lillie is a good listener.
We can do this, and Lillie deserves this! Wish us luck as we

continue on our amazing, fun, crazy, wonderful, exhausting parenting journey, which I wouldn't trade for the world!

MOTHER'S DAY 2016

Max is nine.
Ella is seven.
Lillie is three.

It is Sunday morning and I wake up at 9:00 a.m. Holy cow, a Mother's Day miracle! I think Seth let me sleep, but then realize Seth and Lillie are asleep and Max and Ella are downstairs playing loudly.

Ella hears me coming down the stairs and screams "Happy Mother's Day," and says she wants to make me breakfast. My little tootsie is so sweet. I hate to say no to her. I have been doing a cleanse for two and a half months. I haven't had any sugar. I told myself that today I could finally have a cheat day. I have been wanting a Paula's donut! For those of you who live near me, I know you understand.

Everyone is up and the kids quickly cover me with their beautiful handmade gifts. My eyes are filling with tears when I see the beautiful things they wrote about me. Max and Ella obviously put a lot of work into their gifts. I am hysterical when I see that Ella thinks I was a waitress. Really, Ella? The social work career doing family counseling wasn't as impressive as the waitressing jobs! The things kids say on their Mother's Day questionnaires crack me up!

We all get dressed and head to Paula's Donuts. The line is all the way to the door. We laugh and wait for a long time. Every other mother had the same idea as me! We all want a good donut! We get our donuts and then head to a playground. Seth thought we could go to Kelkenberg Farm, but we are all freezing and not dressed right. I forgot jackets, we aren't wearing pants, and it is a lot colder than we thought. If only we were dressed right, but that would be too easy.

We go home to grab coats and the kids decide they want to stay home. Isn't it Mother's Day? Does anyone care what the mother wants to do? The mother wants to go do something fun. I quickly see that no one is interested but a few of us are hungry and we are out of everything. We go to Charlie the Butcher for some roast beef and Ella can't find anything there she wants to eat. Oh, Ella! If there isn't pizza, mac and cheese, grilled cheese, or chicken fingers we are out of luck with Ella.

We head home and I decide to give up on a fun day and head to Wegmans to grocery shop. We are out of everything and I know I need to pack lunches tomorrow. I finish the shopping and we head to my parents to do gifts on the way to dinner. My mom laughs reading my card, explaining that my brother sent the same card from Virginia! I miss my brother and smile feeling our connection. We both picked the same card for our mom. That is pretty special!

I had a lot of fun shopping for our mothers. Books, garden stuff, a photo book and more. My mother even bought me beautiful gold sandals. She isn't supposed to buy me a present!

We head to dinner with my parents to meet Seth's parents. They give us a high table, but I decide to just go with it. I know this is going to be a pain with Lillie. How many times is Lillie going to get up and down from the stool? How many times will she drop things?

Everyone arrives and we order food. Lillie is begging me for her pizza, and our food is taking forever. Again, I don't want to complain, so I just sit there and bite my tongue. The food finally comes, and I don't like my wings, but I don't say anything. Seth hates when I complain about my food. This place is famous for their wood-fired wings but note to self: I like a traditional wing! It is good to try new things. At least that's what I am telling myself.

We finish dinner and my dad says he wants to go to Pautler's for custard. I see Seth ready to fall over and I decide not to push. It is time to go home. I may not have gotten to do something big and fun today, but I was with my family and that is all that matters!

Happy Mother's Day to me!

WOMEN'S GUILT

If I could do one thing for women everywhere, I would take away your worry and your guilt. No one understands a woman like another woman. Men, I am not trying to discredit you. My husband is amazing! He works a ton of hours to provide for our family and still makes time for our kids. However, I don't see him break a sweat if he misses one of our kids' field trips. I don't see him worrying about our kids the way I do. I am sure there are many men out there worrying and feeling guilt, but this is about women today.

I am going to tell you about one of my friends. She works a high-power job and still makes time for her kids' events at school, for PTA and for Girl Scouts. However, I still see her beating herself up for not being Room Mom, or not being able to stay at a field trip. She took her lunch break to go to the field trip, and still gave herself a hard time for not being able to stay long! She is running to a million kid events and staying up late to accomplish everything that needs to get done, and she is still too hard on herself.

Let's talk about my friend who works part-time. She works, is Room Mom, and does a million school events! I still see her beating herself up for having to miss a field trip. I see these women juggling it all, and doing an amazing job, and still being hard on themselves!

My friend works a lot of hours and has a lot of demands on her, at work and at home. She shows up to lunch duty and apologizes to me that she can't stay long. I see her head spinning. I see the tons of things she needs to get done at work running through her head. I see her stress. She is making time to come do lunch duty to see her kids. Did she give herself any credit that day? I wonder!

What about my friend who told me she was taking the day off for a field trip but couldn't take off for Kids' Day? What about the friend who is sweating over having zero personal days left at work? I feel bad, and I want to get into their heads and switch their thoughts! This is the social worker in me.

I have a friend I see at school dropping off and picking up her son. I see her hurrying to get to work. I know how late she works. I know she still has work and laundry to do after she puts her kids to bed. I see how stressed she is, and I hear her guilt over not being able to take on school volunteer jobs! I want to scream "It is okay" to her. We all do our best. Women have so much to juggle every day! The meals, the laundry, the kids, the house, the job, the pets.....

What about the stay-at-home mom? Let's talk about me. I loved my job. I am a social worker through and through. It oozes out of my pores. At Kids' Day at school my engineer friend was designing hurdles for me, and we had a great laugh as I told her I would be the one busy worrying about everyone's feelings that day. I was doing family counseling, working with families whose children had severe behavioral problems. Then I became a supervisor and got the awesome opportunity to supervise and assist an office of wonderful women doing family counseling. Next was going to be project coordinator or consultant. Many of you know me and know I don't stay idle. I was striving to keep moving up to give myself new challenges. I loved it there and yet the day I looked at Max's face it was all over. I couldn't bear to leave my son! I was crying daily to my husband who wanted me to go back to work but said he would work hard to keep me home.

Let's talk about the guilt that I feel. Am I happy staying home with my kids? Do I love doing Room Mom, PTA Treasurer, Girl Scout leader, softball coach? You know the answer is YES! However, I am not doing my career and I am not helping my husband pay our many bills. Yes, I worry, and yes, I feel guilt!

I didn't even mention my three-year-old. I run to a ton of school things for Max and Ella and leave Lillie with our moms or my friend. I feel the guilt. I feel the judgement I give myself. I tell myself, "Stop running to school and spend time with Lillie." How about if I say something like "Good job juggling three kids. Good job doing things with all your kids!"

Our self-talk tends to be brutal. I have to give myself a pep talk to go out at night when my kids are sad and want me home with them. I need breaks. "It is okay to go out," I tell myself. I feel badly when I am at the dining room table doing PTA work and I am not spending time with my kids. I tell myself, "You're helping your kids' school. It is okay to be doing this work!"

My point in all of this is, women are too hard on themselves and on each other! I would like us all to change our perspectives. Let's look at how fabulous we are. Let's look at all we do. You may not be able to do everything everywhere, but you do enough. You are enough! I think we are all amazing. Let's not judge or criticize one another. Let's cheer each other on and support one another! I say "Women rock," and I am proud of all of us. Rock on with your awesome self! Go tell a woman how awesome she is doing!

Women Rock!

TURNING 40

The day I turned 39 I realized I had one more year in my 30s. It hit me like a ton of bricks. An entire decade was ending! How could this be? I feel like I just turned 30 yesterday. I vividly remember sitting at a big table at Carrabba's with my family and friends to celebrate. I couldn't have been happier (so I thought). I had married Seth in September, so I was 10 months into my marriage. To top that off, turning 30 gave me major baby fever! Seth wanted to have a few years just being married. My response to him was, "Do you know how old I am? No way!" We wanted a few kids, and I was doing the math as to how old I would be having these kids. There I sat celebrating my 30th birthday, two months pregnant with Max! I was over-the-moon excited to become a mom! I was doing a job I loved. I was married to a fabulous man. I was pregnant with my first baby. I was a happy woman! I knew my 30s were going to be awesome!

10 years later, here I sit. I am currently sitting outside at my parents' house. I am watching my brother, son and husband play basketball, and our kids are running around playing. My brother and sister-in-law drove to town with my nephews for my big birthday. They have already made it a special weekend for me just by being here!

I am thinking about turning 40, wondering how these past 10 years went so quickly. I had all my babies in my 30s. Max is now nine years old, Ella is seven and Lillie is three. My 30s were the busiest years of my life. Being a mom is the biggest, hardest, most wonderful career I have ever had in my lifetime!

The difference between turning 30 and turning 40 is a huge one for me. When I think about that 30-year-old sitting there 10 years ago...that woman was clueless! She was clueless as to how busy she was about to be. She was clueless as to how much she would learn and change becoming a mother. She was clueless as to the fact that she would love her husband a million times more 10 years later. I will never forget the day Seth walked me to the bathroom after I had a baby. He was wiping up the blood behind me. No one told me how much you bleed after having a baby! That moment will forever stick out in my mind, as I saw the love and concern on Seth's face. I saw that cleaning up and helping me was a no-brainer to him. Forget the diamonds and flowers through the years. It is the care and love that I treasure the most! Seth, that doesn't mean to stop buying me flowers and diamonds. ;)

I hear all my friends around me cringing at turning 40. On the other hand, the other day a friend posted on Facebook that her brother would have turned 40 that day, and how much she wished he had made it. I am celebrating this birthday! I am happy to turn 40! Don't be shocked. It feels like a badge of honor. It feels like I truly made it through 10 years of motherhood and marriage, doing a pretty good job at both. I am not going to lie. I do screw up every day. I get bitchy to my husband and I yell at my kids if they don't listen. Every day I start over and try to do a better job. I am definitely mellowing with age. The hotheaded 30-year-old is much mellower! I yell less, I get upset less, I care less, I let a lot more go and I say less. I have learned a lot and I am excited to see what I learn in my 40s. I have a strong feeling my 40s are going to be awesome!

I miss having babies, but I certainly don't feel like my kids need me any less. I feel as they get older, they will need me more and differently. Max came to me the other day and said, "You are a social worker. I bet you can help me with this problem I am having." I almost fell over! Then I opened my ears and listened hard to my nine-year-old who needed me. I would like to give you a little research data here. Kids get into the most trouble between the hours of 3-5 p.m. while their parents are still at work. We should all make sure our kids have childcare between those hours! I am certainly going to remember this piece of data as my children get older.

Tomorrow I party! My husband is calling it my Sweet 16 birthday party. I didn't want to stand  in a restaurant drinking and eating. I don't sit still or stand still often. I am going to roller skate with my family and friends to celebrate, and I am so excited! Yes, there will still be drinking and eating. I will let you know how this goes. I hope all my girlfriends will wear age 40 with pride! I am definitely happy that at age 40 I still love putting on a pair of rollerblades!

Happy 40th to me!

WERE WE TAUGHT NOT TO TAKE COMPLIMENTS?

My husband pointed something out to me the other day that really made me think. He said, "Women don't know how to take a compliment." He witnessed one woman tell another that she liked her blouse. The other woman blushed and said, "It's really old." Okay Seth, I get it. Point well taken! I started to take notice:

I have a friend who makes the cutest gifts. Every time we had a PTA meeting, she made the best thank you gifts for everyone. She made teachers these awesome dishes of starbursts with the cutest sayings. I tell her all the time how much I love her ideas. Her response is always the same: "It's just Pinterest!" She may have gotten the ideas from Pinterest, but she always does an awesome job executing them. Haven't you seen people try to copy Pinterest and fail? Others just don't have the energy or desire to do it. Why do we downplay what we do? Why don't we take credit for our awesomeness?

I have a friend who I call the expert spreadsheet maker. She even sent me a spreadsheet for my Disney dining plan! (Thank you by the way xo!) When I tell her she is awesome at spreadsheets and organization she tells me it is just how she relaxes. I tend to lie on the couch watching *The Real Housewives of Orange County* to relax. I do not make spreadsheets or organize my house to relax. She is awesome, my organizational master friend!

259

Yesterday I talked to another friend about private practice. She is a social worker I used to work with. She has been doing private practice for a while and tells me how much she loves it. She says it is like having a conversation. Easy breezy lemon squeezy! She even mentioned working with cutters, and how "easy" it was. Do you know what cutting is? People actually cut themselves on purpose! There are many psychological reasons for this behavior. I am sure my friend does an amazing job with all her clients. I am sure her "easy conversations" are filled with a wealth of her knowledge. Notice she didn't take any credit for her skill and downplayed how difficult therapy really is. It is easy for her because she is so good. Take some credit friends!

My friend who was nine months pregnant stood in my backyard pushing her daughter in a swing. We were all sweating because it was so hot out. She has taken her daughter to camp every day. She has taken her younger daughter to the zoo. She worked the whole school year while pregnant. She just plugs along like it is no big deal. Do you know what I was doing almost nine months pregnant with my children? I was lying on the couch telling my husband I was done and that the baby needed to come out! When I tell my friend how amazing her strength is, she tells me she is just like that. Like it is easy to be tough? Like it is easy to be nine months pregnant in the heat? Nope, not at all! You are awesome friend, and you amaze me!

Another friend seems to go back and forth to work all day. I can't keep up with her schedule! When I ask her to do something, it goes something like this: "I have until 4 p.m. when I have to go back to work. I am going to run and get my daughter here, my son there, and then will you come over? I will order pizza and we can all hang out before I go back to work."

Did you keep up with that? I always laugh and am very impressed. "Okay, I will see you at 1:00 you amazing lady!" I know this friend is running all day every day. I know most of us are. I also know what women are like. We rarely own a compliment, and we rarely give ourselves one. Why is that? I hear my daughter tell herself she looks pretty. I hear my daughter tell herself she did a good job. I am not correcting her. I am not telling her you don't say these things. This is absolutely what we should be teaching our daughters to say to themselves. "Mommy, I really like myself," Ella tells me. "Ella, I am so glad. It is important to like yourself!" My smart girl!

We went to a Lego-themed party yesterday. This mother is amazing. Everything was Legos! Lego chocolates, Lego crayons, Lego treats, Lego props and decorations, Lego necklaces and rings. Everyone was in awe! We all tell my friend how awesome this all is. "Clearly I have too much time on my hands," she jokingly says. Anyone with children has pretty much zero spare time so I know that isn't true. I know she is crafty and talented, and "Wowzers, she needs to plan my next party lol!"

What about my mom? My inspiration! The woman who has been described by many as the Energizer bunny. I get excited if I see her sitting! She taught me stamina. She taught me how to keep up. I often wonder if she realizes how awesome she is. I certainly understand and appreciate her a lot more now that I am a mom!

I hear a lot of compliments given every day. I hear a lot of women underplaying these compliments.

Your crafts are awesome!
Your spreadsheets are awesome!
Your multi-tasking is amazing!
Your stamina is incredible!

Hear it. Own it. Teach your daughters (and sons) to own it! I love the amazing women I am surrounded by!
P.S. I am guilty as charged!

Power on!

ELLA GETS TO BE ANNIE!

I signed Ella up for theatre camp this summer. It is all she talked about the entire summer! Almost every day she asked me what part I thought she would get. Almost every day she told me she wanted to be Annie. My response to Ella was always the same: "Don't get your hopes up." I didn't want her to be disappointed. I figured an older girl would get Annie. I figured Ella would get Molly, the cute orphan. That was my prediction.

The day finally comes, and Ella RUNS off to theatre camp! She is beaming with excitement and my heart is full of happiness for her. When I send one of my children off to school or camp or anything for the first day, I hold my breath hoping for a good report.

I pick up Ella after day one and she runs at me telling me to guess what part she got. "Annie!!!" She screams with delight! No way, I don't believe it. I grab her script to see that she is Annie and my mind is blown! This child has special powers. She put it out there the whole summer and her dream was coming true! You think when you are happy about something, you know what happiness feels like. When one of my children is filled with happiness, it is a new level of happiness for me. I can't stop smiling and am beyond excited for her to tell her dad and grandparents!

We just lost two of our cats and decide to go next door to visit the cat place. Max is thrilled because a certain kitten keeps following and playing with him. The personality of this kitten reminded me of Max. Then I look over at sweet Ella sitting on the floor. The kitten with one blind eye had climbed into her lap and was cuddled up to her. The sweet gentle kitten had chosen Ella. The active kitten had chosen Max. At this point I was trying to control Lillie whose energy was off the charts. Max and Ella are begging me for these kittens. Why did I bring them in here? I knew Seth would not be happy with me if I adopted kittens today, so I drag my children away with tears streaming down Max's face. "Great job in parenting," I tell myself. I should have skipped the cat place. It definitely showed me my children's personalities through kittens. I am questioning myself as I leave but am quickly distracted by the big huge smile plastered on Ella's face.

Ella comes home the next day from camp beaming. She is having the best time, and somehow already knows all her 21 lines and however many songs! "Phew," I tell myself. She has her father's memory. This is going to make life at school and acting easier for her. I am watching her rehearse and begin to tear up. She asks me for a bucket and rag and shows me *"It's the hard-knock life."* This little peanut is starring in a musical!

"Hold on, this is only the beginning," someone tells me. Do you believe in G-d? Do you believe in angels? Do you believe that messages are sent to us? Have you ever asked a question and been answered? I continue to be amazed and my faith continues to grow stronger.

It is now Thursday night and Ella is definitely feeling pooped from a long week. The black shoes she owns don't fit. She doesn't like the two pairs of black shoes I bought her. So off we go for black shoes. Nothing like dragging her out the night before her show! "Way to go doing things last minute," I beat myself up. The second store is shoe success and it is time to go home to let my little Annie rest. She is tired and excited and calm as a cucumber! I could hear my heart beating, I was so "nervexcited" as Ella calls it.

It is the day of the show and Ella is calm, relaxed and happy. I am a nervous wreck and can barely eat anything all day. I am a much better actress then I ever give myself credit for. I act the part of the calm confident mom and send Ella off to camp with a big hug and kiss.

Seth comes home early from work and his look is familiar. He is totally calm and happy. His smile, the way he is looking at me through his glasses....Ella has so much of Seth in her. Yes, she is bubbly and outgoing and social like her mama, but boy did she get a lot from Seth too! "How are you so calm?" I ask Seth. "Help me," I plead to him.

"Rebecca, she knows this. She's got this. She is going to do awesome. She is in her element. What is wrong with you?" Seth asks me. I am holding my stomach. I am nauseous and stressed and nervous for my baby. What do I do in these situations? I turn my worry to faith. Yes, I do! I say a prayer and I tell the tape in my head to turn to faith and confidence in my little actress. Does it work perfectly? No, but I feel much better and drive to the show smiling.

Ella appears on stage and my nerves vanish. I have turned to feelings of happiness and pride! I attempt to make her smile the whole show as she is super serious but knows every single one of her lines. (And everyone else's lines! That is her father in her for sure.) She messes up a song but brushes it off. One of the things I love about Ella is she isn't hard on herself. "What is that like?" I ask myself.

Ella takes the microphone and sings the *Maybe* reprise solo. She sings ALL day at home. Now here she is with a microphone on stage and I couldn't be happier for her! I know that is where she loves to be! This, my friends, is my favorite part of the whole show.

I thought Ella was happy before the show but that was nothing compared to her afterward! The happiness is glowing out of her, and she is jumping and dancing around. She told me she loved every minute of it and can't wait until the next show. When your child finds something they love, it is the best feeling!

What my friends tell me:
"She is going places!"
"She needs her own TV show!"
"Remember us when you are big and famous!"
"She is going to be big!"
What Ella tells me:
"Why won't you take me to Hollywood?"
She also told me her life is the opposite of a hard-knock life!

I don't know where life will take Ella. What I will tell you is if being on stage makes her happy then that is what I wish for her. My little belting dolly shines from within and I wish her nothing but happiness!

Time to go get Ella pancakes to celebrate. I couldn't be prouder! Keep soaring Ella Bella!!

BAD MOMS

Ladies, you all need to go see the movie *Bad Moms*! Go see it with your friends and then take your husband to see it. I went with my friends and I laughed so hard I actually hurt myself! I told my husband how funny it was, and he told me I had to go

 back with him so he could see it. "Twist my arm," I couldn't wait to see it again. But I didn't anticipate what would come from the movie!

Seth and I got a couple's massage, we went out for dinner and we then went to the movies. Trust me when I say this doesn't happen often! It was our eleven-year anniversary and Seth planned a lovely day for us. I was quickly adjusting to actually relaxing. I got to eat dinner without waiting on anyone. I got to eat dinner slowly while having a conversation with my husband. This doesn't happen enough! I thought the evening couldn't get any better and then we went to relax and laugh at the movies.

Seth watched *Bad Moms* and he kept looking at me with this look. He watched the mom's race from one thing to the next and he gave me the look. He watched a mom cry in her van, and he gave me the look. He watched and watched and his appreciation for me grew. He kept squeezing my hand and patting my leg in appreciation. He was seeing my life on a huge screen and he was getting quite the right message. "Wow does my wife work hard," is what he was thinking.

We left the movie and Seth had a lot of questions. First, he told me how much he realizes how hard I work! Then he told me I was the character Kiki which made me giggle. Then he asked "Is that true? Do you feel like that?"

"Yes, yes, yes!" Every mom feels like that. Almost every mom has been by herself in her minivan crying. Almost every mom beats herself up every day. Almost every mom is rushing from one place to the next. Whoever wrote that movie knows how moms feel. I would have thought moms wrote it, but I just looked it up and somehow a couple men wrote that movie! They definitely did an amazing job!

I recently talked to one of my friends about her belief systems. She said her mom taught her that you have to make dinner for birthday parties. You have to cook the spaghetti sauce from scratch. You have to have a big spread. You know what I said to that? "REJECT" that belief system! My amazing mom whips up a spread easily and loves to cook and bake. So do I, but sometimes I am too tired, and that is okay! My brother and sister-in-law have thanksgiving catered. Guess what? It is delicious and easier and good for them! My mother cleans her bathroom every day. My mother cooks every night. Guess what? I reject that! I can't meet that expectation and I am sorry, but I am not a bad mom!

As much as I loved that movie, I did not love the title. We are all in this parenthood thing together. We are all doing it together and doing our best. Yes, we all screw up daily. No one is perfect! Every mom is beating herself up. Instead of giggling and saying we are a bad mom because we just saw the movie, let's all say that we are good moms! Are you doing your best? Are you trying? Let's get rid of the bad mom stuff in our heads and let's call each other and ourselves good moms!

Parent on!

SUMMER 2016

Is it just me or as we get older does time move faster? I swear this was the fastest, most fun summer ever! Ella danced today singing "It was the best summer ever." I truly agree with her sentiment!

I was born on June 25th. It is definitely one of my favorite days. Not because it is my birthday and it is about me. It is my favorite day because of what it represents. Every birthday means success and summer to me. It means my kids successfully completed another grade and summer has begun. It means the weather is beautiful and my parents' pool is open. It means I can take my kids to do a bunch of fun things. It means they can swim and experience fun camps. I truly love summer. The warm weather, the sunshine, flip-flops, sun dresses....my very favorite time of year!

I started out the summer without a bucket list. I feel when you make a list for summer and cross things off it is a lot of pressure. I wanted to relax and enjoy the summer. I signed my kids up for a few camps, and my goal was to take them once to Darien Lake amusement park and do a lot of swimming.

The funny thing is the summer that started out without a list became one of my very favorite summers! We went to my nephew's birthday party in Virginia. We went to Toronto to their zoo and aquarium. (I finally got Swiss Chalet in Toronto!) We took the kids to Jellystone for the weekend with a ton of friends. We took the kids to Darien Lake, the drive-in, Strong

Museum, playgrounds and lots of pools. We spent time with our friends and our family. Max did science camp and ecology camp and loved them both. Ella did theatre camp, cheerleading camp and another theatre camp and starred as Annie in the musical.

It is September 5 and school starts tomorrow! I didn't start out with a list, but there is still a list of things I wanted to do with my kids! We never got to Fantasy Island or Olcott. I never took Max for the hike I wanted to do. I never got to the ropes course my friend talked about. I wanted to go to Hidden Valley Animal Adventure and African Lion Safari. Let's put it this way....I could have filled another month with fun adventures!

I wish I could be that mom excited to send her kids to school. I wish I could say I love this time of year. It just isn't me, and I am not excited. Do my kids drive me nuts? Am I exhausted? Do I need a break? Yes, yes, yes! Every year I am sad summer is over and every year I am sad to send my kids back to school. That is just who I am, and I accept myself for who I am. I don't judge the mom dancing down the driveway as the bus leaves with her kids. I think "Good for you! I am glad you are happy and getting a break."

Every year we all get back into the routine with ease and have a good year. I couldn't be more thrilled with the teachers my kids have this year. My son is starting fourth grade and believe it or not it is his last year of elementary school. My friends are already asking me how many times I will cry this year. Didn't I just send Max to kindergarten? Ella is going into second grade and Lillie is starting UPK (Universal Pre-kindergarten).

To the moms who dance down their driveways as their kids leave: "I am happy you are excited. I could learn from you!" To the moms crying that their babies are going to kindergarten or middle school or high school or college: "You have done a great job with your kids and they are going to soar! Have faith in your parenting and in your children and know that they've got this!"

I wish everyone a fabulous school year ahead. While I am very sad that summer is over, I am excited to see my kids grow this year. What they learn and say continues to amaze me! Have a great school year and continue to be amazed by your children! For those of you very sad that school has begun, I hope you can take comfort in knowing that you are not alone!

MISTER MOM
BY SETH GREENE

I attempted to do everything my wife does in a day. Key word is "attempted." Why would I do such a crazy thing?

She had continuing education for her social worker license, so she was going to be at "work" all day.

So, I thought I would try and take her place, in case she ever went back to work before Lillie hits kindergarten. That won't happen as we only have one year left, but she's always telling me that if I tried to do what she did, I would fall over.

Spoiler alert: I fell over. Multiple times.

Plus, she even helped me, so I didn't have to do EVERYTHING.

She made the lunches for all three kids the night before. Then she woke up early and packed all their backpacks. She laid out all their clothes. She wrote me out a detailed itinerary of who needed to be where when.

So, what did I do?

Somehow, I managed to sleep through my alarm, as for some reason the kids did not wake me up.
I don't understand this, as every other day when Rebecca is home the kids get me up early. The one day she's not here and I actually need to get up, they let me sleep.

Not so late as to make me late for anything. That would not have been pretty.

I woke up and fed Max and Ella breakfast.
I got them dressed (well, Max dresses himself).
I brushed their teeth.
I attempted to do Ella's hair (sorry Ella, not my best dad talent).

Then Lillie woke up. I threw her in the car in her pajamas and no shoes and took Max and Ella to school. Luckily, we left at the right time for drop-off.

It's all about what time we leave the house. Leave at a certain time, and there's no one in line, and you are in and out in two minutes. Leave a few minutes later and there are 10 cars ahead of you, plus the caffeine-addicted moms who are trying to turn left into Tim Hortons, thus blocking the left turn lane into school.

Seriously? You can't go with the light? Or get coffee before you go into the circle? Thanks Timmy Ho. I suggest we take up a collection to buy the two houses next to Tim Hortons and bulldoze them so there is more room for the line of caffeine addicts.

I've never been a coffee drinker, but if I have to keep being Rebecca, I might start.

Lillie and I come home. I make Lillie her morning breakfast shake, following the recipe and the ingredients laid out by Rebecca.

I vacuum the living room.

I sweep every room downstairs.

I attempted to empty and load the dishwasher. I never succeed because I always load it wrong (according to Rebecca).

I played dolls with Lillie.

I get her dressed.

I brush her teeth.

I attempted to do her hair (sorry Lillie). Even Daddy's ponytails are lame.

I drive her to her friend little Ella's house. We pick up Ella. I drive them to UPK. I meet their teacher (who I haven't met yet) and drop them off.

I drive to Kinko's to pick up some stuff I need for my upcoming conference in Las Vegas the next day.

I drive to work.

I have a meeting with my staff.

I bring in a new client.

I reply to emails.

I coordinate a client's book launch – he hits #25 on Amazon on day one, and #2 on day two!

I go to the gas station as I am now on empty.

I see why Rebecca has three times as many miles on her car as I do, when we leased them the same month.

I run home to get a fleece in case the kids want to play on the playground in the cold.

I go to UPK. I pick up the girls. I drive them to little Ella's house.

Lillie and Ella decide to have a contest to see who can hold on to the hand-grip the longest. Lillie loses and starts crying and screaming.

Then they have a contest on who has a fancier dress on. Ella insists hers is fancier because it is purple. Lillie starts screaming.

I end the contest and start a Barbie music sing-along.

Everybody's happy again.

I drop Ella off at her house.

I race to school to pick up Max and Ella.

It's rainy and cold so I avoid the playground.

We head home.

Mean Daddy makes them do homework as soon as they get home.

Rebecca gets home from training for five minutes before she is going out with friends for dinner.

As I am leaving for Las Vegas at 5 a.m. the next day and am leaving her to prep for Lillie's birthday party by herself, I figure I shouldn't complain.

One of her friends drops off her daughter, who I am watching so they can go out to dinner.

The kids play happily together (thank G-d) until Rebecca gets home from dinner and the mom takes her daughter home.

Then we get the kids ready for bed.

Rebecca wants to tell me about her training, and I make myself listen for a few minutes before I pass out to get my few hours of sleep before my trip.

Holy Cow!

Lessons learned:

If you are going to do that much driving, you MUST have a car charger for your phone. I did not.

Watch your gas gauge – I see now why Rebecca doesn't realize she's on empty, and it seems like she's on empty at least once a week, probably more, I just don't know about it.

Bring protein bars in the car – I never had time to eat lunch. The 90 minutes Lillie is actually in school (because you need time to drive back and forth), isn't enough time to get much done.

You basically have time to get one or two errands done before you have to go get her.

Is it time for kindergarten yet?

It's exhausting – I should have skipped work and taken a nap for 90 minutes.

I don't know how Rebecca does it.

So, I raise a glass (with lots of alcohol) to all you super moms out there. Have a stiff drink and a massage and a mani-pedi, you deserve it!

MY DISNEY TRIP AND TIPS

The last time I went to Disney World my son Max had just turned one years old. We had the best time! Max loved everything and I couldn't wait to take him back. Unfortunately, it took us nine years to get back. Somehow, Max is about to turn 10. Time has gone way too quickly!

If you want to take a relaxing vacation, I would advise against Disney World. I decided that since I remembered very little, I would take a Disney prep course that I designed for myself. "What did this course entail?" you are probably asking yourself. It started with my friends who had recently been to Disney or who go there frequently. One of my favorite ways to gather information is to ask my friends for advice and tips. I met with my friend Laura three times to help learn about Disney and plan my vacation. She gave me tons of information and I am beyond thankful to her. I think she should switch careers and be a Disney travel agent! Laura, I seriously can't thank you enough. I also asked Sarah, Angela, Kristin, Karin, Kimberly, Jennifer....you get the drift!

I bought an awesome book to read about Disney and bought one for Max and Ella to read too. My kids loved reading and learning about Disney World. Let's not forget the hours on the internet looking over Disney information. You have to get the *My Disney Experience* app. It was so helpful! I decided I was going to learn about Disney, and I was going to plan a great trip for my kids. I was on a mission! (I tend to speed fast ahead with my missions.)

For those of you who know very little about Disney like I did, Disney offers a dining plan. You get to book one sit-down meal a day and you also get a snack and a quick service meal (per person). I knew my girls would LOVE character meals, so I immersed myself in learning about each meal. Ella had her heart set on eating at Cinderella Castle. No pressure! I only heard that was the hardest meal to get. Everyone was right!

You can book your dining six months ahead if you stay on a Disney property. Seth and I got up extremely early the morning we could book our dining. We were heading to Disney on December 11th and leaving December 15th. I was going to start with the Cinderella Castle meal and look on every day and every meal to see what I could get, which was hard. Phew, I got a lunch for December 14th! This was by far our favorite meal and favorite experience. The castle is gorgeous, the view is so cool, the princesses were all great and the food was so good! I can't recommend this meal enough.

I also booked Akershus in Epcot, which was a great one too. My girls met princesses and the food was delicious. We went to Hollywood and Vine for lunch in Hollywood studios. This was a buffet. The food was okay but Lillie, my four-year-old, bounced the whole meal with glee as Sofia, Jake, Handy Manny and Doc McStuffins came to our table! We went to Tusker House in Animal Kingdom. This was also a buffet and we didn't really like many of the food options for this meal. Seeing characters was fun though!

Finally, I booked *Be Our Guest at Magic Kingdom* for lunch, which was another meal I wanted to try. My friend Laura taught me that you can pre-order your food ahead of time. I am so glad we did, because they took us in so much quicker than the people who had to place their orders. The castle was very cool, but I wasn't impressed with the food. I would love to try dinner at all these places, but it was hard enough to get lunches. I was also traveling with seven people which makes it much harder to book meals than a smaller party. I still want to try Crystal Palace next time and many others!

Do you know about fast passes? If you have gone to Disney, you are saying "Of course I do!" This is something I had to learn about. You can book three fast passes per person per day for whatever park you are going to. The fast pass line is super-fast, and the standby line can be super-slow. The standby line for the *Frozen* ride in Epcot was two hours long. You want to book fast passes! I booked mine on my *My Disney Experience* app.

I read about each ride and asked friends a lot of questions. I have to be very careful because my daughter Ella hates rides and gets scared very easily. My family is not into big rides and is not into roller coasters. You have to tailor your Disney plan based on what your kids like. After you use your three fast passes, you can look on your app on your phone for what other fast passes are available, and you can keep booking them all day one-by-one. I loved this feature! There were also kiosks where you could do this. You also want to make sure you build your fast passes around meals and parades and shows you want to see. I knew we had a 1:00 lunch and a 3:00 parade, so we did rides around that.

Let's talk about having three very different kids. I wanted a family vacation. Sure, Seth and Max went to a couple rides by themselves, like the Haunted Mansion. However, as much as possible, I wanted to stay together as a family and experience Disney together.

Max is nine, Ella is seven (and hates rides), and Lillie is four. There are height differences and different desires I had to take into account each day. I tried my best to make all my kids happy. I had a talk with them that I wanted this to be a family vacation, and we would take turns doing what everyone wanted to do. I asked them each day to pick one thing they really wanted to do that day. I felt one thing per child per day was easily attainable, and then I added to it from there. If your kids don't know anything about Disney just pick things you think each child will like. Max really wanted to do *Soarin' Around the World* at Epcot and the girls really wanted to do the *Frozen* ride, so we split up and accomplished both of these! They are both a tier one fast pass pick, so we had to split up for that. You definitely want a fast pass for *Soarin'* and *Frozen.* We loved *Frozen* and wanted to go back on again, but the wait was two hours without a fast pass. That is so nuts! Ella didn't love it as much as Lillie and I did. Ella was much more interested in the character meals and the shows and would have skipped all the rides.

Our favorite rides:
I have to do *It's a Small World* when I go to Disney. So cute!
Peter Pan was awesome!
Winnie the Pooh was so cute!
Pirates of the Caribbean was cool!

Buzz was cute and you have to do *Dumbo*!
Toy Story at Hollywood studios was a lot of fun!

My friend Kristin gave me such a good tip to put a scarf on my stroller. It helped me so much to find my stroller. First, a ton of people had the same stroller as us. Second, the people who work at Disney kept moving my stroller! Seriously. They kept trying to straighten and make room and kept moving my stroller. In a sea of strollers make yours easy to find! One woman told me she thought it was easier to bring two umbrella strollers than a double stroller. Not a bad idea but then Seth and I are pushing a stroller all day and I liked taking turns!

We loved Epcot and only had a few hours there. Next time I want a full day there! Hollywood Studios was so fun and so was Magic Kingdom. I could have skipped Animal Kingdom and will skip it next time. It was just okay. Max really enjoyed it, as I knew he would. Next time we want to add Universal Studios, Sea World, a water park and I still want to see Downtown Disney! I have never done that.

More notes for myself for next time: While I can handle a 9 a.m. to 11 p.m. Magic Kingdom day my children (and husband) cannot! Next time I would go in the morning to Magic Kingdom, go back to the hotel for lunch to swim and rest, and then go back to Magic Kingdom for evening rides and the nighttime show. If I plan a day this way, we get to swim in the hot sun and avoid the busiest time of day at Magic Kingdom. It is much easier to get on rides in the morning and evening than it is in the afternoon.

Max loved a lot of the rides. He doesn't get scared easily but does not like major roller coasters. He definitely could have done Splash Mountain and the Seven Dwarfs mine train. I will book those for him next time to do with Seth and I will go take the girls to go do something else.

Don't forget about yourself! The two things I forgot to pack were for me. Also, I wanted to see the parade and no one else did. Guess what? They stayed and watched the parade with me because as my friend put so well: what Mama wants counts too!

How to stay sane: I told myself sleep and relaxation was for when I got home! When my children or husband were overheated, I found things where we could sit in air conditioning. A perfect example is *Mickey's PhilharMagic*. It was an adorable show, and we needed to sit and chill out with AC.

My favorite tips:

Laura: Character meals, *My Disney Experience* app, you have to try dole whip (awesome snack), book fast passes one at a time after you use your first three. (Pre-book these!)

She gave me so many tips! She also told me you could buy groceries and have them shipped to you at Disney. We didn't do this but maybe next time? Laura also taught me about the Magical Express and shuttles. We stayed at *Art of Animation* on Disney property. It was amazing! A food court, themed rooms, huge pool, shuttles to all the theme parks, and a great store.

When you stay on a Disney property you get to book your fast passes and dining before others. You also get to use the Magical Express. We took it from the airport to our hotel and then hopped on a shuttle to Epcot. Our luggage was waiting in our room when we got back! When we were leaving the hotel for the airport, the hotel took our luggage to the airport for us, we took the Magical Express to the airport, and our luggage met us at home! Amazing! The books were an awesome tip too. Laura was my travel agent!

Kristin: Scarf for your stroller to find it. I know she gave me many tips, but I'm so thankful for this one!

Sarah: Pay attention to where you book your fast passes so you can get to all the rides in time. Clothes for all types of weather. You really don't know how it will be. Cold? Hot? Raining? I brought rain ponchos too. We didn't need any cold weather or rain gear, but I never would have known that! Sarah also told me about some great websites she uses.

Seth: My husband said to forget fashion and wear sneakers. Tons of walking! He was right. Yes, Seth, I did just say that. :P

Al: My father-in-law said to bring bathing suits. I almost forgot this, and you never know how the weather will be. It was so hot, and I am so glad I brought them! The kids swam every day.

Angela: For Jedi Training at Hollywood studios you have to get to the park early, to wait in line to get on the list. I got there at 8:30 and they let us get in line at 8:45. The line was huge. FYI, I also read your child who is doing the Jedi training has to

MY DISNEY TRIP AND TIPS

be with you when you sign them up. It's for ages 4-12, and the child has to be able to follow directions.

I didn't sign my girls up because I knew Darth Vader and Kylo Ren would scare them. Angela was also so helpful in knowing my kids and what rides they would like!

Jen: Bring special Disney surprises to appear on their beds each day. Great tip! It is fun for the kids and you save money this way. I actually didn't get to this. I let each child buy one present while at Disney. (I may have bought them a few more things, and I also bought myself a couple things!)

Jennifer: Have each child pick one thing they really want to do for the trip. I decided to do one per day.

My main goals for the trip:

Ella: To eat at Cinderella Castle. I also knew Ella would want to see shows so I made sure to do that for her!

Max: To do *Soarin'* and Jedi training. He was a little too old for the Jedi experience, but I am glad he got to try it! I wish I had taken him a couple years earlier. I knew Max would want different things than the girls, so I made sure to check in with him each day on what he really wanted to do. The poor kid met so many princesses. He is such a good big brother! Major points to Max for tolerating so many princesses!

Lillie: She just wanted to meet all the characters and I knew she would be the easiest kid. She loved all the rides and all the characters. She was so happy! I am still glowing from watching Lillie giggle and smile so much!

I have such good friends! Laura, Sarah, Angela and Kristin have gone to Disney a lot and could answer all my questions. I had a lot of questions! Thank you, friends for being so patient with me and for teaching me so much! An enormous thank you to my father-in-law for taking us on this magical adventure! Huge thank you to my husband for humoring me and keeping up with my Disney madness! It was a lot of work to plan but was so worth it. I wanted to write down tips for myself to remember and for my friends who are currently planning their first trips to Disney. You are going to have a magical time! I loved it so much!

MARKETING LESSONS FROM DISNEY WORLD

I couldn't have been more excited to finally take our kids to Disney World. I just wanted to go have fun with my kids and then Seth said, "Take notes of marketing lessons you can present!" What? He wants me to "work," and he wants me to present what I learned? I used to present all the time. I used to run meetings. I used to do trainings. I was feeling rusty, but I would give it a try for my husband. It was easier than I thought to find lessons to teach people for their business.

The first question I asked my children when planning for this presentation was "How did you know you wanted to go to Disney World?" They talked about Disney all the time and asked us frequently when we could go. Both Max and Ella agreed they wanted to go to Disney World because their friends talked about it. Disney sounded so awesome to them and they couldn't wait to go. They also watched a ton of YouTube videos on Disney.

What are the lessons here for your business?
1) You want people talking about you in a positive regard and you want people referring their friends to you. The biggest tool in marketing (from this mama's perspective) is word of mouth. If my friends say someone or somewhere is amazing, that is all I need to know. How are you getting people to refer to you? Are you encouraging your clients to refer to you and giving them an incentive to do so?

2) How are you utilizing YouTube for your business? My kids and I are on YouTube. Your business needs to be there, if it isn't already!

How can you make your clients' lives easier? I was so impressed with Disney World and the ways they made my trip easier for me. I went to the airport and checked my luggage, and later that night my luggage appeared in my room at Disney World. The luggage piece was amazing in itself and made my life with three children so much easier. When I got to the Orlando airport, the Magical Express was there to take me right to my hotel. When we got to our hotel, we jumped on a shuttle to go straight to Epcot. The transportation services were so awesome! I loved that I didn't have to worry about my luggage or transportation.

The other way Disney made my life easier is through their app, *My Disney Experience*. I had booked our fast passes 60 days ahead of time. However, after you use your three fast passes, you can add one at a time depending on what is available. There were kiosks where you could add fast passes, but I had the app and could add fast passes on my phone all day. As we were standing in line for one ride, I was booking our next ride. How can you use an app to make your clients' lives easier? Everyone is on their phone all the time. Use this phone fact to your advantage!

My girls were all about meeting the characters at the character meals. My son was such a good sport about this. He really let his sisters have fun. At our first restaurant, we saw Snow White, Aurora, Ariel, Cinderella and more walking around. I quickly realized the princesses had a system of moving around the restaurant so they made sure they got to every table. I could just sit and relax and enjoy my meal and I didn't have to worry about my girls  meeting every princess. How are you making sure all your clients are getting the services they need? How are you making it fair, and making it so they don't have to worry about you covering everything you need to cover for them? What is your system?

I have heard so many people tell me Epcot is for adults. A lot of people told me not to bother taking my children there. However, Disney is brilliant, and they moved Elsa and Anna to Epcot. My girls also kept asking me to take them to the new *Frozen* ride that was in Epcot. I am very impressed with Disney making an "adult" location more child-friendly. Max loved the ride *Soarin'* and Ella and Lillie loved the *Frozen* ride. We didn't get to spend a lot of time there so next time I want a whole day in Epcot. How can you make something that isn't so desirable more desirable to your clients?

Our friends explained to us that we want to get to Hollywood Studios before it opens, so we could get in line to sign Max up for Jedi training. Max got to be on stage and be a Jedi in a show. It was very cute. Not only do they let kids be a Jedi, they are also building a *Star Wars* section at Hollywood Studios to capitalize on the current craze. Disney is so smart!

Focus on what is popular and bring it to your theme parks. How can you bring what is popular into your business? How can you use *Frozen, Star Wars*, etc. to appeal to your clients? I saw an awesome car commercial that utilized the *Star Wars* craze to their benefit!

I have already briefly mentioned the character meals. My girls were so excited to meet all the princesses. My four-year-old, Lillie, went nuts when Princess Sophia and Doc McStuffins came up to her. When I saw their excitement, it made me think about how Seth and the rest of you could use this to your benefit. We were more interested in the characters than we were with the food. What about having meals with your clients? Who can you bring to these meals for your clients to meet? Do they want to meet you and your staff? Are there local celebrities you could book to come to your meal? What about having a princess meal for your clients' little girls and hiring Elsa and Anna to come?

Do you know what your clients are interested in? Do they like to read? What do they like to read? You could send them a free book to let them know you are thinking of them. Do they love Disney World? Do they know you just went to Disney World? If you know what your clients interests are then:
1) They feel more engaged with you and feel like you care about them.
2) You know what to talk to them about.
3) You can use their interests in their business. For example, if you do social media for them you can use their interests in their marketing.

The *Indiana Jones* Show at Hollywood Studios was even better than I remembered it last time. This time there were narrators that helped to take us behind the scenes of the stunts. What happens at your office? How can you show your clients what is happening behind the scenes? I know that if I saw how hard you were working for me as your client, and what you were doing for me, then I would be happier with the services you provide for me.

The special effects at Disney World were awesome. My girls loved that it rained on stage during *The Little Mermaid*. They loved that bubbles were everywhere in the theater during *Finding Nemo*. They were ecstatic when it snowed in the theater during the *Frozen* Singalong. It made me start thinking about how you can use special effects in your business. Do you have special effects in your office? I know my brother has a very cool waterfall in his office that I always stare at. What about special effects in the videos, websites, marketing you do for your clients?

My son loved being a Wilderness Explorer in Animal Kingdom. He ran through the park trying to find the places where you can earn a sticker/badge for his book. There were staff members present at different locations in Animal Kingdom to teach the kids something so they could earn a badge. Max was so engaged in not only this process but also in finding the hidden Mickeys all over the parks. This made me think of two things for business purposes. First, how can your clients all earn something? What can you engage them in, so they earn a grand prize? Also, what about team building and client engagement? Could you get your clients all working toward earning badges to engage more with your services? You could give out prizes along the way. What about getting your staff together to go do a scavenger hunt for a team-building exercise? Max loved hunting for hidden Mickeys.

Make sure you are giving your clients what they want! I booked us a meal at Tusker House in Animal Kingdom. My kids loved meeting all the characters, but the food was African-themed. Nobody was thrilled with the food at Tusker House. We still had a good time, but it made me think that we have to make sure we are giving people what they really want!

Make sure your clients and staff have all the information they need. I am so unimpressed with our travel agent. I asked her questions, but she didn't really offer me much information. When we got to Disney World and tried to use our Magic Band for a meal, they asked us for our pin. What on earth is a pin and how do I get one? When I tried to get my girls a pretzel the next day at Hollywood Studios the woman asked me for my pin. I told her I thought we straightened this out last night. She sent me to guest services and they quickly resolved this issue. The pin was definitely information our travel agent should have given us. Hopefully you have a checklist of everything to go over with your clients to make sure they know everything they need to know!

The customer service at Disney World was magical! I couldn't have been more impressed with them. You want your clients to say this about you! When I wanted to get my girls a pretzel, I was frustrated that my pin still wasn't working to use my Magic Band. The woman saw that my girls were hungry. She saw that I was frustrated. She handed me the pretzel and told me it was on Mickey. That was so sweet of her and I will remember that.

My father-in-law and I thought something was wrong in our dining plan points. We went back to our hotel to check before we went to the Cinderella Castle for lunch the next day. The man at the desk explained to us that we thought we had a five-day dining plan, but only had a four-day plan. He explained that you can only have dining when you are staying in a hotel that night. He was so sweet, and he told us the Cinderella meal tomorrow was taken care of. He gave us enough points to eat at the castle with no hesitation. I was so amazed by this. I would go back and stay at the *Art of Animation* again because they are so good to their customers!

A friend asked me to get her Mickey hair extensions when I was at Disney. I checked every single store and was so frustrated that I couldn't find them. Finally, the last store I checked had the hair extensions. I was so excited! The woman cashing me out saw how excited I was. She told me, "The hair extensions for your friend are on Mickey and take one for your daughters too!" Can you believe this? Have your clients rave about you the way I am raving about Disney World!

The first night we were in Disney World we were all tired. We had flown to Orlando, gotten on the Magical Express to our hotel, and then got on a shuttle to Epcot. I didn't expect all of us to last long at Epcot. Ella and Lillie were dying to go on the *Frozen* ride, and I couldn't get a fast pass until 9 p.m. I saw my girls fading and I tried to get in line twice for the fast pass and got turned away. I told the woman my girls were exhausted, and she told me to go ahead and get in the fast pass line. The standby line was two hours long so there was no way I was getting in that line. I later learned that you can't use your fast pass until five minutes before your assigned time. I was so touched that she let us get in before our early window. You want to say "yes" to your clients as much as possible. Saying yes to people leaves them with good feelings about you. Say yes as often as you can!

The decorations at Disney World were gorgeous! They beautified Disney World and made it so welcoming to be there. I was happy to be there just to get to look around and see everything. How can you dress up your home or your office to make it more inviting to people? Disney World knows what they are doing!

There are so many business lessons to learn from Disney World. These were just a few things I noticed while I was there. I hope you can learn something for your business from my observations.

FEELING LIKE A FAILURE

It was Thursday night and my family was sitting down to dinner. I was feeling so sad as we all ate our food. I couldn't shake this feeling of wanting to cry. I was trying to figure out what was wrong with me. My kids finished eating and asked to leave the table. My husband and I finished eating and I stared at all the dishes in front of me. I started bawling right at the table. My husband looked over at me concerned, waiting to hear what was wrong. "I feel like such a failure this year!" There it was, it came out of me without my knowing what I was going to say! Now I knew what was wrong with me all day. Actually, that is what was wrong with me all week.

Seth looked over at me like I had 10 heads. He couldn't imagine how on earth I could be feeling this way. I knew he was confused so I told him I would explain. My schedule is completely different this year. Nine-year-old Max and seven-year-old Ella go to school all day. Lillie is four and goes to Universal Pre-K. She got into the afternoon spot, so she goes to school from 11:50-2:20 every day. It works really well for her. She can sleep in and relax and then get ready and go to school. I get Seth and the older two kids out the door and then I work on getting Lillie ready. We fight about her clothes, we fight about her eating something, and we fight about a lot of things in the morning. Lillie is my baby, my sweet cuddler who also knows exactly what she wants! I have to give her clothes options, or she flips out. Then she heads to my vanity and starts doing her makeup! Yes, you heard me, she wants to put on makeup every day! I don't even care at this point, because trust me when I say I pick my battles with this one! Then Lillie asks me to do her nails (every day) and then she asks me to do her hair (exactly how she wants it). After this long routine I drag her downstairs and begin the food battle of trying to get her to eat something before school. She is never hungry before school and I usually try to get a smoothie into her. Before I know it, it is time to get Lillie to school. I now have two hours to fit in errands, laundry, dishes, cleaning, and working out! You can imagine how quickly the two hours go by. The next thing I know I am picking up Lillie and then Max and Ella. You all know the drill after school with kids: homework, activities and dinner are now ahead of me. The next thing I know it is 7:00 at night and I am wondering where the day went!

So, there I sat at 7 p.m. crying to my husband about feeling like a failure. I was feeling this way because my days were flying by. I was feeling this way because I couldn't possibly fit everything I wanted to do into my day. I was feeling hopeless and sad about what my days were looking like. My days were being sucked up from me.

"Stop right there," my husband says. "Are our kids happy and healthy? Are they doing well? Are they thriving? This is your life this year. It is okay! There is nothing you have to do except keep them happy and healthy. You are doing great! You are so not a failure! You are succeeding at your job and you don't see it!"

There are times I would wallow in my sadness. This was not one of those times. He is right! My kids were doing great at home, at school and at their extracurricular activities! Why was I being so hard on myself? Why do I do this? Why do I always feel like accomplishing things gives me worth? I don't have to accomplish things. I have to take care of my kids and BE with them! I need to sit down and play with Lillie instead of doing laundry. I need to be enjoying every minute with Lillie! Do I find her to be difficult? Yes! Am I going to cry when she goes to kindergarten? Yes! If my days are flying by, I'd better start enjoying them!

Put down the dishes. Put down the broom. Put down the work you brought home. Put down your phone and go be with your family! Read a book, play a game, watch a movie. We don't have to always be DOing something! Just BE with the ones you love! I have some shifting to do!

Lesson Learned!

I am going to go put down my phone and watch *Wreck-it Ralph* with my family!

SEPTEMBER GETS CRAZIER!

I am going to be brutally honest with you. September makes me want to stab my eyes out! Just when I think it can't get any busier, it does. Somehow, every year, I make it through September.

Let's start back in July. My kids were out of school and we were having a great summer. However, despite happy July, I was going to bed worrying every single night. I knew September was going to bring a ton of changes and I was finding myself holding my breath thinking about it! Wouldn't it be nice if I could just learn to go with the flow?

When September 5, 2017 rolled around, my 10-year-old son Max was going to start middle school! He was leaving his elementary school bubble and stepping into a new world. I was mostly excited for him. I knew he was ready for a change. Change is exciting but it is also scary to me. My mind wasn't consumed with worry for Max, it was with another one of my children.

Ella was starting third grade and Lillie was going to be starting kindergarten! Max and Ella were both well over five when I sent them to kindergarten. I was sending my baby to kindergarten at four years old! Everyone had an opinion whether we should send her or not. I kept telling myself to send her. I kept convincing myself she would be fine. She would turn five on October 2nd. "That is only a month after school starts," I would tell myself. Let's be honest here, I was so worried! Was I making the right decision? The bottom line is there isn't a right or wrong decision about this. There is just a decision. I decided to send her. Again, I was holding my breath!

I had a wonderful summer, but I spent a lot of time worrying about Lillie. She went to Universal Pre-kindergarten last year, which was only two and a half hours a day. I couldn't imagine how she was going to do six hours a day! She was so used to being with me. How was she going to do without me all day? She is my baby! That alone makes it so much harder to send Lillie to kindergarten!

I decided to leave my job to stay home with my children. I've devoted 10 years to staying home with them. My whole world was about to change! As I saw it, my career was ending. I spent many days crying. Even if I continued to be a stay-at-home mom, it was going to be very different. I don't have any more babies and I was grieving. I had so many friends tell me to have another baby. I love babies! I wanted four babies! But after three C-sections I couldn't get myself to go through another one. Seth was so done having babies. There was no use trying to convince him, because in my heart of hearts I was done too, and I didn't want to be!

The first day of school came like it does every year. Max and Ella did such a great job getting Lillie excited for school! I sent Max off to middle school excited, I sent Ella off excited and I even sent Lillie off to school excited. I did a wonderful acting job and left my girls at school happy. I would now hold my breath until I picked Lillie up. How was this going to go?

I am writing this on September 16th. I feel this huge sense of relief! Max is getting the hang of middle school and Ella and Lillie are loving school! That's right, Lillie loves kindergarten. Do you have any idea how wonderful it is to say those words? Lillie LOVES kindergarten!

As parents, you know there are a million things to do. You know you have lists that are a mile long. You know once one list is finished another one quickly emerges. Let's just say that when the kids go to school, I have had no trouble adjusting to not having kids at home during the day! Another shocker for me!

When you take on a job you never realize how much work it will be. This is something I have come to learn. When I took on the membership job at my girls' school, I had no clue what I was in store for. September has gotten significantly crazier! Let's throw in activities for all three kids, three different school open houses, two Jewish holidays, and company for eight days!

So, when you ask me what I am doing with my free time, I haven't found any yet! However, I am hopeful for October! When I find some free time, I will let you know what I do.

ANOTHER MINIVAN

My lease on my car was up and I was determined not to get another minivan. I was ready for a change. I have had three minivans, and although they are so convenient, there is no fun factor. I love cars and I wanted something fun!

A friend said she hated her Acadia, but that's what I had my eyes set on. I was going to get a pearl white Acadia with tan seats. I had my mind made up and that was what I wanted!

I had an Acadia dropped off at my house. I was determined to get my family to love it. All three kids and my husband got into the car and made a face! I asked them to give it a chance and off we went to soccer. I loved driving it, but then we pulled into the parking lot. I grimaced as they opened the doors praying they wouldn't damage another car or their fingers! I guess I have been spoiled for nine years with my sliding minivan doors.

We watch Max's soccer game and then head back to the car. Seth makes a face as he tries to fit all our chairs in the trunk. "This trunk sucks!" he tells me. I am driving home and Max is telling me he is getting carsick. "Mom, I don't like this car! I want a minivan! The minivan is our home on wheels. Why would you ruin that?" Ella is in the third row complaining about how uncomfortable she is back there. Lillie is in her car seat smiling, telling me how cool this car is. Thank you, Lillie! At least one of my family members agrees with me!

They didn't know it, but they brought me the exact Acadia I wanted. It was a beautiful white with tan seats. I stared out at my driveway, knowing it wasn't going to be mine. As much as I would like to put myself first, we all know where this is going. "Mom, I am carsick! Mom, I am squished! Rebecca, this trunk has no space! Kids, be careful with the doors!" All these things were playing in my head.

Seth and I head to Toyota to get another minivan. "I am at least getting a white one with a tan interior!" I tell Seth as I mope to the dealer. "You are being a spoiled brat," Seth tells me as he looks over at my sad face. Yes, he was right. No, I didn't want another minivan. The dealer tells us, "We have a blue or black Sienna in the model you want to pick from today." I didn't want to come back. I didn't want to order a white one. "Let's just get this done and get the black one!" I am so done!

So here I sit in my black minivan. I have been moping about it for three months now, but today I had an epiphany. I am a mom! I am a mom who loves her kids and puts her kids first! That is what this minivan stands for. Today I will smile and drive my minivan!

SUMMER SADNESS & SICKIES

Summer started out great! My son couldn't have been happier to be done with fifth grade. Ella was sad to leave her sweet teacher and Lillie felt the same way. We were ready to party. My family loves the summer! Our summer tends to include the usual bucket list of pool hopping, lunches out, camp fun, s'mores, Niagara Falls, Darien Lake, Fantasy Island, the drive in, and lots of fun family time. I love having my kids home. I am that mom that cries every September when summer ends.

This is how our summer started. Seth left for a work trip to Vegas in early July. We are always sad when he leaves but we are used to it. He doesn't enjoy leaving us, but Seth loves his work trips. He gets to be around people who think like him. He gets to learn a lot, teach a lot and get more clients. I was happy to hear he was enjoying his trip, but I was home very sad watching my 16-year-old cat slip downhill. I was trying to prepare myself but how do you prepare to lose one of your very best friends?

I found my cat Hope when she was a tiny kitten. I am a social worker and I was counseling families in their homes. I went to my client's house on Buffalo's East Side, and Hope came up to me outside their house crying for food. She was so tiny and pitiful, and I didn't want to leave her on the streets. I went home that night hoping the whole night that she would be there the next day. She was. My client's daughter caught

Hope for me, and I put her in a carrier and brought her home. I didn't even know she was all white because she was so dirty. The poor baby was starving and had three different types of worms. I fixed her all up and kept her and loved her for 16 years. I named her Hope because I hoped all night that I could find her and save her. That little kitten saved me! We saved each other! I was in a bad relationship at the time and I cried every day and she comforted me and loved me as much as I loved her. We both fell for Seth and then she put up with my three crazy kiddos. She didn't love to be held. She only wanted to be petted and her favorite thing was for you to just sit next to her.

Seth flew home from Vegas to an unhappy wife. I took Hope to the vet and got the bad news that her kidney disease had progressed. I took her home knowing that I would have to go back to the vet. I couldn't get her to eat or drink. I couldn't get her to move. She sat in her favorite corner of my bedroom and stared at the floor for hours and hours. I went to bed that night and woke up to find her in her same corner staring at the floor. I knew this was the end and Seth went with me to the vet to say goodbye. Welcome home Seth!

We left the vet, packed up the car, and drove off to Virginia to meet my new niece Minka. In all my grief and sadness, I kept telling myself I was going to go hold my new niece. Seth drove straight for seven hours as I sat there crying. I couldn't have gotten away from my house fast enough. I wasn't quite sure how I was going to go home.

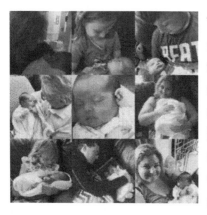

The next day Seth was off to my brother's charity golf tournament. It was a rainy cold day and Seth was not a happy camper. I spent the day holding my niece and trying not to cry the whole day. Being with my family was the best medicine that weekend. I didn't want to get in the car to go home but it was inevitable. I had to face that Hope wasn't going to be waiting for me when I got home.

Seth went off to work and arrived home that night complaining about his forehead. He thought he had gotten hit in the head with a branch at the golf tournament. I touched his forehead and the cut seemed to be moving. I was totally freaked out and made him go straight to Urgent Care. The poor man had shingles. How the heck do you get shingles? Oh yes, you get it from stress!

Seth was in a ton of pain and miserable and Max was grieving the hardest of all of us and was begging me for kittens. If my plate wasn't full enough, Lillie woke up with pink eye! Where did she pick that up? She proceeded to have a fever and feel bad for about a week!

At this point, Seth wasn't feeling well, Lillie wasn't feeling well, and Max was in total sadness grieving Hope. He couldn't handle not having a pet in the house. We were visiting cats and getting lots of cat love at shelters. Crazy Mommy here decided to foster kittens to make Max happy! I just wanted to see him smile and cuddling and playing with a kitten.

Now Ella falls ill with a fever, and one of the kittens isn't acting right. The kitten goes off to the vet for a couple days with a kitten virus. Lillie and Ella get better, the kitten comes home, and Max decides it is his turn to be sick. Do they have to take turns? Normally when Lillie is sick, I keep Max and Ella away and we are safe. Not this time. This time, they fell ill one-by-one like dominos. I got on the phone and cried to my mom, and then decided I had to go with the flow.

Here I am today venting out all my frustrations. I have a husband who is improving but still not feeling well. I have a son who is still complaining about his stomach. I have a bigger kitten who is too rough on the smaller kitten. Day by day I am getting through it all. If you ask me how my summer was, I will probably laugh. I don't care about Darien Lake or the beach or summer fun. I care about my family.

I will tell you that in all of this my priorities have changed, and I have slowed down. I don't feel the need to run around. I don't feel the need to fit everything I possibly can into my summer. I feel the need to appreciate this wonderful family that I have created. I pray every day for their health and their safety. A good friend told me all of this is fixable. That is what I am thankful for. Everything is fixable and time will heal all of this. There are people who can't say that.

I want to say thank you. Thank you for my amazing hard-working husband who has worked many hours while not feeling well. Thank you for my three healthy children who will all feel better. Thank you for these two little fur balls that have brought lots of love and energy into my home. I'm not sleeping as much, and I feel like I have two more children, but I love these little kittens. They have really helped us with our grief! Thank you for my health and ability to care for all of them through all of this. Summer 2018 has taught me to appreciate things differently. It wasn't an easy summer. It was a summer that taught me to slow down and smell the roses.

ANXIETY SETS IN

Now that you've heard about my awful summer, filled with sickness and the loss of my beloved cat, I want to go into more detail about how I coped and share what helped me, because it may help you as well.

I don't tend to suffer from anxiety. My anxiety tends to be situational when I do have it. I have felt the pull to go back to counseling. My plan in my head is private practice for my future. Anxiety is one of the most common complaints I will get from my clients. I started to realize that all this anxiety I have been feeling over the last several weeks was going to help me understand my clients better. When they come to me suffering from anxiety, I would have a better understanding of what it feels like. It wasn't fun, but I learned what worked for me to help and I want to share.

When I am stressed, I tend to wake up with anxiety. What I found was if I got up and moving, it would decrease. If I stayed in bed and tried to rest and relax or go back to sleep it would get worse. Being up and moving helped me. I think if I would have even gone on the treadmill or outside for a walk that would have been even better!

There are many more things that helped me besides getting moving. Awareness is the key to success. First, I started becoming more aware of my breathing. I hold my breath a lot when I am stressed. Thinking about my breathing and taking deep breaths would help me. If you breathe in for the count of one and breathe out for the count of three, and repeat this a few times, you will notice a significant difference. I never want to downplay how important it is to take deep breaths when you are stressed!

Let's go beyond breathing. Let's go a step further, to becoming aware of your thoughts. My negative thoughts were spiraling out of control. I would remind myself that everything was fixable. My kids and my husband and my kitten were all going to feel better. I would shift myself to focusing on everything that I was thankful for. It is much harder to be upset when you are feeling thankful. My husband has been cranky for four weeks, but he will be okay. He will heal, and he will feel better and he will be less cranky!

I don't know what you believe in, but I find that prayer really helps me. I started a cute little prayer that makes me giggle every time I say it. "I will hold out hope and I will keep the faith." Every time I say this prayer I smile. My cat's name was Hope and my new kitten is Faith, so I have created a prayer with their names to warm my heart.

I have mentioned moving, breathing, changing your thoughts and prayer. When I say get moving, it doesn't have to be exercise. I found jumping into dishes and laundry made me feel better. Instead of sitting and wallowing, being productive made me feel better. When you become more aware of your thoughts you can do a better job working on replacing them. When I would think "worst summer ever," I would challenge myself and work on replacing this thought. Not only would everything be okay, but I started to look around and notice what my children were doing. I would find Lillie playing with her kitchen giggling and laughing. I would find Ella playing with her Barbie or on the floor with a kitten giggling. I would find Max cuddling with a kitten or "yelling at" his friends on the Xbox. Yes, I like to get Max out and away from electronics. However, if I actually became present and looked around, I would see all happy children with no one complaining!

I can't emphasize enough how important it is to use your supports. A friend scolded me for not sharing with her everything that was going on. I didn't want to bring people down. Why was I looking at it like that? Friends are for the good times and the not-so-good times. Friends help you through things. I would want my friends to lean on me so why wasn't I leaning on them.

When my friend showed up with coffee and a hug, I felt a million pounds of stress melt away! Use your supports. Lean on your supports. I have a fabulous friend who drove Lillie around for me when Max and Ella didn't feel well. I have friends and my in-laws checking on us. I have parents not only listening to me vent daily but also supporting me and loving me and giving me guidance through it all. My parents have a health food store and would show up with stuff regularly to help us through this. Marlene and Phil's Vitamin and Herb Center is the BEST! Check them out: facebook.com/MarlenePhilsVitaminHerbCenter/

My parents do so much research and always find the greatest things to give to my family. I vented to my mother a billion times through all this. I can only hope Seth and I are as good of parents as mine are. When you become a parent, you become a parent for a lifetime. I have had to explain to Lillie many times that she could be 80 years old and she will always be my baby!

My kids love the Holderness Family. We put them on, and dance and sing and laugh and be silly together! You cannot be anxious or upset when you are dancing and singing with your children! My kids now tell me to go drink my chardonnay. You will only understand this if you have seen the Thanksgiving episode of the Holderness family. (Since this blog post was written, Seth actually had the chance to do a podcast with them! What a thrill for him, and for our family!)

Everyone has a creative outlet. Ella loves to act. The emotion she puts into her acting just astounds me. Lillie loves to draw. I find her drawing all the time. I like to write. I cannot tell you how much better I feel when I put all of this to paper. I read my blog post about summer 10 times. Every time I read it, I took a deep breath and found myself feeling much better. When I get it out onto paper it seems to get out of my system! Whether you use a pen and paper or a laptop, try venting out your frustrations. It is the same thing at night. If there is something bothering me or something I don't want to forget before I go to sleep, I write it down. I get it out of my system and then I am able to go right to sleep.

In sharing all of this I hope that I have helped someone!

Get moving. Exercise or be productive!
Deep breathing!
Meditation!
Become aware of your thoughts and challenge/replace them!
It takes practice!

Thankfulness! What are you thankful for? You can't be upset when you are feeling thankful!

Prayer!

Use your supports! Accept help, vent, and ask for advice! I have a few friends who know a lot about cats who have been very helpful. My parents' knowledge about supplements has been extremely helpful.

Put on music and sing and dance!

Creative outlet: painting, drawing, writing, acting....

I hope you are all having a good summer. I hope you are looking around and smelling the roses. I hope if you ever suffer from anxiety that this will help you.

MY DOG TANNER

I grew up with dogs. My life started with Gretel, then came Pandy, and then came Suzy and Belle. Suzy was my black lab that I remember picking with my father. Suzy is the dog that I miss every day. She was the driving force behind my yearning for a dog of my own! My brother's sweet dog Kingston, my neighbor's dog Jackson, and my friend's dog Cooper were also reminding me how much I love dogs!

When I met my husband Seth, he had two cats and I had one. I did not grow up with cats. My parents do not like cats. The only reason I had a cat was because I found her on the East side of Buffalo during a home visit while I was working. She looked so pitiful that I wanted to bring her home and save her. We loved our three cats. One by one they all got old and passed away. We were all devastated, and my son was begging me daily for kittens. Persistence tends to work, and my son got his way. My husband wasn't ready for more animals, but we were already fostering two kittens that he knew we were going to adopt. I'm sorry we did this so quickly Seth. I was putting Max's needs ahead of yours and I apologize for that!

I started to tell my husband that if we were going to get a dog that now was the time. He had held me off for many years because I didn't want to disturb our old cats. I didn't know how they would take a new puppy in the house, so I decided to wait. Now that we had two young kittens, I figured that kittens and a puppy growing up together was the best way for them to get used to each other. I didn't want to wait until the kittens were cats and were more set in their ways. My husband was not amused with me.

I mentioned getting a dog several times over the next few months after we got the kittens. My daughter Ella would cry telling me that she was afraid of dogs. I told her she didn't know what she was missing because she has never had a dog! My son Max and daughter Lillie told me they were happy with their kittens and didn't want a dog. Seth was feeling extremely annoyed with me feeling like I was never happy. Seth loves to sing the song Never Enough to me from the movie The Greatest Showman. It drives me crazy.

I started to realize that I was the only one in the family that wanted a dog. I didn't really care. Sometimes it is about mama. Sometimes mama gets what she wants. I started to look at rescue sites online every day. I fell for a couple of dogs that were quickly snatched up. I started to realize that it was not that easy to get a dog. The application process on these rescue sites were intense. We were a nice family who was going to provide a good home for a dog. I couldn't believe the process I was about to go through to get one. I also was quickly getting disappointed every time a dog I liked got adopted. This was not going to be as easy as I thought it would be.

One day my husband Seth came up to me and told me that he thought that we should get a dog. I couldn't believe the words I was hearing. I was completely and totally floored once again by my husband. As you probably read in my last blog post, I don't always know what Seth is going to say. He can be very unpredictable. Seth was feeling very sad that the kittens weren't bonded to him. The kittens love all of us but they love Max the most. They are really Max's kittens. He picked them, he named them, and they seem to know this. They love their mommy, but if they could talk, they would tell you that Max is their favorite. Seth knew this and he felt like it was time for him to get a buddy.

Our friend Rachel posted her puppy Millie on Facebook. Millie is a gorgeous Golden Retriever. Seth showed me Millie's picture and told me that if he was going to get a dog, this is the dog he would get. He didn't realize that I then messaged Rachel to ask her where she got her puppy. I couldn't even believe it when she told me that she got her from a breeder in Amherst (ten minutes away), and that the breeder had one male puppy left! If Seth was going to get a dog, he was going to get a Golden Retriever male dog. He told me he preferred a one year old dog to skip the puppy phase! However, I told him this new information that I had received about this puppy! I was now getting texts from the breeder asking me if we would like to come meet this puppy. Seth agreed, and the next day we went to go meet our dog!

I did not expect Seth to say yes to getting this puppy. I was preparing myself to go meet the puppy, have a good time, and then go home without the puppy. Again, my husband likes to surprise me. Seth met our dog and instantly fell in love. I could not believe it when he told me that he wanted to get the puppy. I just couldn't believe it. He paid for our puppy and we arranged for a time to pick him up after we bought some supplies. I was in complete disbelief. After all of these years of trying to convince Seth that we needed a dog, he was finally taking the plunge!

I felt sad that I didn't rescue a dog from a shelter, but I strongly believe that this happened how it was supposed to happen. This was our dog! This woman ten minutes from our house had one male Golden Retriever left and he was our dog! She met us and instantly knew that this was our dog. There were no questions, no application, no home visit, just a nice lady seeing a nice couple who was about to give one of her puppies a wonderful home.

The next day, after getting supplies for our puppy, Seth ventured off to pick up our dog. He walked through the door and surprised all three of our children. We all instantly fell in love. My sweet Ella who was afraid of dogs had no problem falling head over heels in love with her puppy. I can tell you that she loves him the most! Now it was time for a name!

My children's names are Max, Ella and Lillie. I wanted a T name so that I could spell the word MELT with their names. As corny as that it is, that is what I wanted and that is what I was going to get. My cat was Hope so Max named our kittens Faith and Joy after Hope. It was time to get my T! As I was talking to my sweet little puppy, I called him Tanner. I knew that was his name. He looked like a Tanner. Ella has added Alexander as his middle name (she just saw the musical Hamilton about Alexander Hamilton so this is appropriate coming from Ella). Tanner Alexander Greene (TAG), welcome to our family. You are crazy, you are a lot of work, and we are all in love with you!

CLOSING THOUGHTS

I started writing my Whinypaluza blog when Max was six years old, Ella was four, and Lillie was 10 months old. Fast forward six years later and I have a 12, 10 and six-year-old. I started writing as a mother of very young children. At that point in my life Lillie wasn't letting me sleep through the night. Max had just finished kindergarten, Ella was in preschool, and Lillie was walking around while holding onto things. Life was so different back then. It feels like so many years ago and also feels like a fast blur.

My family has been through so much since I started writing. I feel very blessed to have so much of our busy life documented. You will see there are times over the last six years when I was writing, and times when I wasn't writing. There are lapses in time. I didn't keep up with it on a weekly basis like I had planned. If I have learned anything in the last six years, I have learned to be easier on myself. It is okay that I didn't write every week. I just feel fortunate for the blog posts I did write.

When I started writing I was a completely different mother. My life completely revolved around my children. I was lucky to squeeze in a shower and rarely put on makeup. I was sleep deprived and had Lillie sleeping in our bedroom. We lived in a smaller house with three bedrooms. Max and Ella's bedrooms were small, and I didn't want to shove a crib in either of their rooms. I also didn't want Lillie waking up Max or Ella during the middle of the night, so her crib lived in our bedroom. I remember shopping for our current house for six months.

I hope you laughed and related to Seth and I as you read through my blog posts. We really do our best every day to keep up with our children. The biggest changes in our family were moving to a bigger house and losing all three of our elderly cats. As you read, we now have three new fur babies. Our two kittens are Faith and Joy and our puppy is Tanner.

I have changed so much as a mother over the last six years. I started out as a mother who could only live for my kids every day. I did everything for them and wanted everything to be as perfect as possible for them. I felt guilty every time I did something that didn't have to do with my kids. If I went out at night, I felt guilty. If Seth and I went to a hotel for an overnight, I felt guilty. I felt guilty if they cried because I wasn't home. I was striving all day every day to give my children the best possible life I could. I was a complete and total people pleaser who wanted my children, my husband, my parents, my friends, etc. to all be happy. Not only did I want them to be happy, I wanted them to be happy with me.

Six years later I am a completely different woman. Six years ago, I was 36 years old, which makes me 42 as I write this. My 30s were completely rocking and busy as I had my babies. I had Max at 30, Ella at 32, and Lillie at 36 years old. Every decade we learn and grow so much. I was so ignorant in my 20s. I got smarter in my 30s but was completely wrapped up in having my babies. The woman I see in the mirror at age 42 is a different woman.

I have learned a few very important lessons. Lesson number one is that it is time to worry about myself more. I have always told women to take care of themselves, but I have never really owned it for myself. I didn't necessarily think that applied to me. Now I have realized that if I don't take better care of myself, I am not a good wife or mother. I get cranky and irritable and yell a lot if I don't worry about myself. I need time to exercise, read, write, get my nails done, get a massage, etc. If I take more time for myself, it makes me happier and a much better person in general.

Seth travels for work. He goes to conferences and speaks at them and learns a lot and makes a lot of business contacts. His latest trip was the first time I was home alone with three children, two kittens and a new puppy. When he came in on Thursday night, he made a date with me for Friday morning to go out to breakfast. We got the kids off to school and then Seth asked me to head out to breakfast together. I sat on the floor and cried like I have never cried before. I had held it in for years and years and finally let it out. I try to be strong and be super woman every day. I had completely and totally crashed. Seth has never seen me cry like that. It was at that moment I owned that I wasn't taking care of me. You are going to hear more about how I take better care of myself, so I don't end up sitting on the floor crying hysterically. It doesn't have to always be about everyone else.

Lesson number two is that everyone doesn't have to be happy. I don't have to say yes to everything. I don't have to sign Lillie up for every activity she asks for. I don't have to say yes to every birthday party the kids get invited to. I can say no to my kids and I can say no to everyone around me.

Those are just a couple of the lessons I have learned in the last six years. You are going to hear more about my children. You are going to hear about my son's Bar Mitzvah that is next year. You are going to hear about my fur babies and our first time having a puppy. I grew up with dogs, but this is the first dog for Seth and I. You are going to hear about our parents, our friends, and adventures in teenager land. Max as a 12-year-old is completely different from Max as a six-year-old. I look forward to continuing to write and take you on more Greene adventures.

I hope you enjoyed this book, but it's only the first one. More to come! My blog will continue, and I hope you will continue to follow us. You can find my latest blog posts at whinypaluza.com. I appreciate all your love and support. The biggest advice I can give you is to remember to take care of yourself! If mama isn't happy, nobody is happy!

Laughing, Loving and Learning,
Rebecca Greene, LCSW-R

Rebecca Greene

To Contact Rebecca Greene:
Email: becgreene@hotmail.com

Made in the USA
Middletown, DE
13 September 2021